The Animal Rights Debate

ISSUES

Volume 169

Series Editor

Lisa Firth

D1421983

Independence

Educational Publishers
Cambridge

First published by Independence
The Studio, High Green
Great Shelford
Cambridge CB22 5EG
England

© Independence 2009

British Library Cataloguing in Publication Data
The Animal Rights Debate – (Issues Series)
I. Animal rights II. Firth, Lisa
179.3

ISBN 978 1 86168 473 8

Printed in Great Britain
MWL Print Group Ltd

Cover
The illustration on the front cover is by
Don Hatcher.

CONTENTS

Chapter One: Animal Welfare

Chapter Two: Animal Experiments

Chapter Three: Blood Sports

Useful information for readers

Dear Reader,

Issues: The Animal Rights Debate

There is much debate surrounding animals' rights. Is fox hunting necessary to control a farming pest, or a cruel blood sport? Is it acceptable for animals to suffer painful testing in order to find cures for debilitating human illnesses? Intensive farm practices cause animal suffering but also provide cheap food, relied on by many poorer families. These and other dilemmas are looked at in detail in **The Animal Rights Debate**.

The purpose of *Issues*

The Animal Rights Debate is the one hundred and sixty-ninth volume in the **Issues** series. The aim of this series is to offer up-to-date information about important issues in our world. Whether you are a regular reader or new to the series, we do hope you find this book a useful overview of the many and complex issues involved in the topic. This title replaces an older volume in the **Issues** series, Volume 103: **Animal Rights**, which is now out of print.

Titles in the **Issues** series are resource books designed to be of especial use to those undertaking project work or requiring an overview of facts, opinions and information on a particular subject, particularly as a prelude to undertaking their own research.

The information in this book is not from a single author, publication or organisation; the value of this unique series lies in the fact that it presents information from a wide variety of sources, including:

⇨ Government reports and statistics
⇨ Newspaper articles and features
⇨ Information from think-tanks and policy institutes
⇨ Magazine features and surveys
⇨ Website material
⇨ Literature from lobby groups and charitable organisations. *

Critical evaluation

Because the information reprinted here is from a number of different sources, readers should bear in mind the origin of the text and whether the source is likely to have a particular bias or agenda when presenting information (just as they would if undertaking their own research). It is hoped that, as you read about the many aspects of the issues explored in this book, you will critically evaluate the information presented. It is important that you decide whether you are being presented with facts or opinions. Does the writer give a biased or an unbiased report? If an opinion is being expressed, do you agree with the writer?

The Animal Rights Debate offers a useful starting point for those who need convenient access to information about the many issues involved. However, it is only a starting point. Following each article is a URL to the relevant organisation's website, which you may wish to visit for further information.

Kind regards,

Lisa Firth
Editor, **Issues** series

* *Please note that Independence Publishers has no political affiliations or opinions on the topics covered in the **Issues** series, and any views quoted in this book are not necessarily those of the publisher or its staff.*

A moral claim not to feel pain

Intensive farming and the use of animals in the entertainment industry raise even more pressing ethical questions than the use of animals in biomedical research

By Lisa Bortolotti

The view that animals have moral rights is a difficult one to accept because of the widespread assumption that moral rights come as a package: either you have none, or you have them all.

As it seems laughable to suggest that a chimpanzee should enjoy the right to an education, or the right to freedom of expression, then it is assumed that he should not enjoy any right whatsoever.

A chimpanzee can feel pain, and has an interest in not feeling pain

But it is possible to justify the right of any mammal not to have pain inflicted unnecessarily without also defending their right to vote at the next election.

That is because a chimpanzee can feel pain, and has an interest in not feeling pain, but cannot decide between the domestic policies of rival political parties, and has no interest in doing so. We do not frustrate any of the chimpanzee's preferences by not allowing him to vote, but we do frustrate his preference to be free from pain if we kick him around for no reason.

From the very origin of the idea of rights and consistently in the development of this idea, the entitlement of an individual to respectful treatment has been justified on the basis of whether the individual has preferences and acts on those preferences.

If the possession of those psychological capacities determines who has rights, shouldn't we be open to extending rights to non-humans, provided that they can also exercise the same capacities to some extent?

We can describe some animals as agents with preferences: chimpanzees have preferences about what to eat and where to live – although they do not know they do.

On the other hand, we might have no reason to believe that they have plans for the future or beliefs about their own existence. This suggests that they do not have an interest in their continued existence and that there are no grounds to accord to them a right to life.

These considerations, as any other in moral decision-making, should of course be weighed up with other moral considerations before giving rise to decisions or actions.

Should we stop experimenting on primates if that would slow down scientific achievements that could lead to the development of treatment for debilitating diseases? These questions are difficult, because they require us to weigh up the morally relevant interests of individuals who are deserving of careful moral consideration, i.e. the primates used in research and the people awaiting a cure.

Before we can answer questions like this, we need to know more about the case. Would the primates involved in that particular research project be subject to pain? How likely is it that the research project would give rise to a potential breakthrough? Could the experiment involve other species of animals, less sensitive than primates to pain and stress, or could it be done in ways that do not require any animal to suffer?

Although we do not know a lot about the mental life of other animals, we do not need to know a lot about it before we can speculate that they have an interest in avoiding pain. Good evidence comes from their behavioural responses to potentially painful situations and from physiological similarities in pain perception mechanisms between humans and non-humans, especially in other mammals.

This makes it harder for us to justify current human practices involving other animals, where these animals are treated in ways that are likely to cause them considerable pain. Intensive farming and the use of animals in the entertainment industry raise even more pressing ethical questions than the use of animals in biomedical research, because the outcome of these practices has a more tenuous contribution to make to interests that are relevant to our well-being.

In conclusion, some animals can make a moral claim on us not to be inflicted pain, even if it does not make much sense to accord to them the full range of so-called 'human' rights. As long as they can be shown to have preferences that have an impact on their well-being, those preferences deserve moral consideration.

28 February 2008

⇨ The above information is reprinted with kind permission from the New Statesman. Visit www.newstatesman.com for more information.

© *New Statesman*

Gana the gorilla: grieving mother?

Information from *The Scotsman*

By Richard Bath

It was a poignant scene which reduced many onlookers to tears. Gana, an 11-year-old gorilla at Germany's Munster zoo, cradled her dead three-month-old son, unable to accept that he had died in her arms. Yet no matter how tenderly she nudged, caressed and cuddled the lifeless form, there was no movement from Claudio.

She carried his corpse everywhere, guarding the little figure so zealously that wardens at the zoo were unable to retrieve the dead baby gorilla for four days. But it wasn't her anger that left a lasting impression; it was the rawness of a mother's pain. So clearly inconsolable, bewildered and shattered, her face displayed a range of emotions that we once thought of as uniquely human. This week she was a grieving mother first, an ape second.

Gana demonstrated, movingly, just how alike gorillas are to us. They live in sophisticated social groupings with complex, hierarchical structures and are known to mourn the loss of their young. The American anthropologist Dian Fossey, who devoted her life to the study of lowland gorillas, even witnessed them burying their young by shovelling leaves over their corpses.

The DNA of gorillas and humans is 99.9% identical, yet it is one thing to accept in theory the extent to which we are related to the great apes, quite another to witness it. 'Many of the visitors were terribly shocked,' said the director of Munster zoo, Joerg Adler. 'This, perhaps, is one of the greatest gifts that a zoo can bestow: to show that "animals" are very much like ourselves, and feel elation and pain. Gana lost a child, but I think in that loss, she taught people here so much.'

Is this really true? Do we actually believe that gorillas are so similar to us that there's an equivalence in our feelings? Or are we just fooling ourselves? Did Gana simply show us that apes are sentient beings worthy of being treated as such, rather than as dumb animals?

Like virtually all our cultural mores, our attitude towards animals has been defined by faith. Religions differ profoundly in their approach to their relationship with animals: the Hindus believe all animals have the capacity to be reincarnated as a human; while India's Jains go further, believing that all living beings possess a soul so all life is considered worthy of respect, even the life of a fly, which is considered sacred.

Traditionally, Christianity is diametrically opposed to that view: humans are the only beings to enjoy free will, the only beings to possess a soul (even though the Latin for 'soul' is 'anima', the derivation of animal). 'Thomas Aquinas and the scholastic tradition said very clearly that animals have not got souls and this has been used in the past to justify the exploitation of animals on the basis that they are just things,' says John Austin Baker, the former Bishop of Salisbury and a prominent animal rights activist. It remains the prevailing view in the West. In one survey, just 19% of British vets agreed that animals have souls.

The DNA of gorillas and humans is 99.9% identical

Yet there has recently been a profound sea change in Christian attitudes to animals. In 2000, Pope John Paul II created uproar in the Catholic Church by decreeing that 'also the animals possess a soul and men must love and feel solidarity for our smaller brethren'. Society's attitude towards animals is also changing, and there is little doubt why. Darwinism was the first scientific challenge to the concept of the dumb animal, but ever since *The Origin Of Species* holed the creationist myth beneath the waterline, the weight of scientific evidence suggesting animals have a previously unsuspected range of emotions has stacked up.

Instinctively, we know that Greyfriars Bobby possessed sentiments such as loyalty, devotion and the pain

of loss, but more quantifiable animal emotions are also being revealed. Just last week came evidence that chimpanzees who have spent time in vivisection laboratories suffer from post-traumatic stress disorder exactly as humans would.

In 2004, researchers at the Babraham Institute at Cambridge University proved that when sheep were isolated from their flock they experienced stress, while showing them pictures of sheep reduced their stress levels. Dr Lynne Sneddon at the University of Liverpool has published research which comes close to proving that fish feel pain, while Prof Kevin Laland of St Andrews University showed that fish have long-term memories and sophisticated social skills.

'We are living through an ethical revolution when it comes to animals,' says theologian Andrew Linzey, an expert in the ethics of animal welfare at Oxford University. 'We are shifting from seeing them as objects, commodities, resources, to seeing them as beings in their own right.'

While there are obvious differences, the debate on the degree to which animals are sentient beings is in some ways reminiscent of the process that brought the end of slavery and the emancipation of women. Slavery began to unravel in 1772 when black slave James Somerset successfully argued in a British court that he was a sentient being who should be accorded rights rather than viewed as property. Campaigners seeking female emancipation followed the same tactics, establishing a wife's right to be a being in her own right, equal with her husband when it came to important functions like voting and divorce.

One sure sign that society's attitudes towards animals are changing is the creeping use of a politically correct vocabulary of parity to describe the relationship between man (or 'human animals') and animals ('non-human animals'). In American officialdom and at England's DEFRA, the word 'pet' has been replaced by 'companion animal', suggesting some sort of meeting of equals.

This creeping de facto change of the status of animals is being consolidated by a series of law changes which may

have profound long-term consequences. The Animal Welfare Act 2006 doesn't just require pet owners to give their animals a suitable environment, a healthy diet and protection from injury and disease, but also to cater for their pet's emotional needs, including 'the desire to exhibit normal behaviour patterns' and be 'housed with, or apart from, other animals'. Failure to comply can carry a £20,000 fine and/or a custodial sentence.

If attitudes towards animals in general and great apes in particular are changing, as shown by the ban on fox-hunting and medical experiments on gorillas, chimpanzees and orangutans, we are still lagging behind some nations. The EU accepted as long ago as 1997 that sentient animals are those which can not only suffer physical pain but mental trauma, an important legal precedent. In New Zealand in 1999, a coalition of scientists and lawyers only narrowly failed in its attempt to get parliament to go one step further by extending rights to large primates. In Spain, it will be two months tomorrow since the country's Parliament passed a law giving great apes a whole range of legal rights.

The trend is exacerbating our tendency towards anthropomorphism – the allocation of human traits to animals.

Occasionally this has tragic results. Timothy Treadwell wanted to prove that bears inherently share our values of loyalty and friendship, so went to live among them in Alaska. It was a triumph of hope over expectation that lasted 13 years until Treadwell and his girlfriend were eaten alive, a story that inspired Werner Herzog's award-winning film, *Grizzly Man*.

This anthropomorphism extends to regarding an animal's death as we would the death of a human being. Researching her book, *Goodbye Dear Friend: Coping with the Death of a Pet*, author Virginia Ironside discovered

endless epitaphs, like this one, published in an 'In Memoriam' column in *Dogs Today*: 'Shayne 1972 – June 90. I can't believe it's two years since you left me, but in my heart you live on for ever. We have 18 wonderful years together. You helped me grow up and taught me so much with your love. We will be together soon, wee man. Wait for me, son, love Mum XXX (Michelle)'

But there are moral problems with the prevailing trend. If we no longer see animals as our property to do with as we wish, then it becomes very difficult to sustain the case for killing and eating them. That is certainly the case for many of the 12.5 million British vegetarians who refuse to eat meat. Inspired by Australian activist Peter Singer and his seminal 1975 tract *Animal Liberation*, animal welfare organisations have long argued that our level of civilisation is determined by the degree to which we treat animals as equals.

For the silent majority to whom the ideas of animal rights activists such as Singer are anathema, the ending to Nim's story was telling. So, too, is a detail of Gana's story which emerged in Munster this week. Far from being the ideal of the doting mother, last year she rejected her six-week-old daughter Mary Zwo, who is now a star attraction at Stuttgart zoo.

Would most human mothers in similar circumstances do likewise? For the moment, it seems, some animals are still created more equal than others.

24 August 2008

© *The Scotsman*

Animal welfare in the UK

Information from the RSPCA

Eight out of 10 people believe that animal welfare is a key priority for a civilised society, according to new figures produced by the RSPCA – compared to just five out of 10 who believed it two years ago.

In addition, almost six out of 10 shoppers are now concerned about animal suffering when buying chicken – as many as those expressing concern about human rights or the environment.

The figures are part of an annual study conducted by the charity to determine how much animals are suffering or being exploited in England and Wales.

'These figures are extremely impressive as they show that the plight of animals is a hot topic at the moment,' said David Bowles, the RSPCA's head of external affairs.

'The campaigns led by Jamie Oliver and Hugh Fearnley-Whittingstall earlier this year mean that higher welfare chicken is literally on the tip of people's tongues.'

Areas of major concern

Many figures are not as positive, however, and reveal some areas of major concern.

⇨ The number of dog fights being reported to the RSPCA has become 15 times more prevalent – up from 24 to 358 – since 2004.

⇨ Despite recent improvements, 85 per cent of chickens bred for meat are still raised in poor conditions, and 62 per cent of eggs are still produced by caged chickens.

⇨ Nearly 30,000 reptiles caught in the wild were brought into the UK last year – a fivefold increase since 2000.

⇨ At least a fifth of dolphins and porpoises washed up on our beaches are killed by fishing nets.

⇨ Around 3,000 primates are used in experiments every year in the UK – and 10,000 in the European Union (EU) – a figure that shows no sign of reducing.

Measuring animal welfare in the UK

The annual report entitled *The welfare state: measuring animal welfare in the UK* is the RSPCA's unique and groundbreaking snapshot of animal welfare data.

Each of the 'animal welfare indicators' in the report measure a year-on-year change using a system of green, red and amber traffic lights to show whether animal welfare has improved, deteriorated or remained the same.

In the latest 2007 report there are five green lights, five red and 18 amber. There are also five grey lights, which show that at present there is insufficient or no data available to accurately measure the indicator, but where the RSPCA believes there should be.

'While the public are clearly concerned about animal welfare, this report shows that there are many areas in which we need to vastly improve,' said David Bowles.

'We've all got an animal welfare footprint – whether we be individuals, governments or organisations – so we need to seize the moment, make the changes that people are crying out for, and ensure that we are the generation that delivers dramatic improvements in the way we treat animals.'
10 November 2008

⇨ The above information is reprinted with kind permission from the RSPCA. Visit www.animalwelfarefootprint.com for more.
© RSPCA

Animal Welfare Act 2006

Information from DEFRA

When did the Animal Welfare Act come into effect?

From 6 April 2007 (and in Wales from 27 March 2007), animal welfare law was improved.

Not only is it against the law to be cruel to an animal, you must also ensure that all the welfare needs of your animals are met.

What does the Animal Welfare Act do?

It makes owners and keepers responsible for ensuring that the welfare needs of their animals are met.

These include the need:

1 For a suitable environment (place to live).
2 For a suitable diet.
3 To exhibit normal behaviour patterns.
4 To be housed with, or apart from, other animals (if applicable).
5 To be protected from pain, injury, suffering and disease.

The law also increases to 16 the minimum age at which a person can buy an animal and prohibits giving animals as prizes to unaccompanied children under this age.

Anyone who is cruel to an animal, or does not provide for its welfare needs, may be banned from owning animals, fined up to £20,000 and/or sent to prison.
15 August 2008

⇨ The above information is reprinted with kind permission from DEFRA. Visit www.defra.gov.uk for more information.
© Crown copyright

The fur trade

Information from Animal Aid

Victory! In the UK, farming animals to kill them for their fur was banned and finally phased out in 2002. Fur farming still goes on around the world and fur garments can still legally be sold in shops in the UK.

So why do tens of millions of fur-bearing animals die every year just to make fur coats?

There are two simple answers: profits and vanity. People who kill animals and make coats out of their skins make money out of it, and people who wear the coats think they look glamorous. The fur trade tries to advertise fur as 'natural' to hide the horrific and unnatural way that the animals are imprisoned on fur farms, or trapped in the wild, and then killed.

Worldwide, more than 40 million animals are killed for their fur

Fur farming

Worldwide, more than 40 million animals are killed for their fur – 85% are bred and killed on fur farms and the rest are trapped in the wild. This figure does not include the thousands of millions of rabbits killed for the fur trade. The most commonly bred animals on fur farms are mink and fox, but the industry also breeds and kills polecats, raccoons and chinchillas. It is estimated that two million cats and dogs are also killed for their fur. There are 6,500 fur farms in the EU. Europe is responsible for 70% of global mink fur production, and 63% of fox fur production. The countries that farm the most animals for their fur are Denmark, China and Finland.

The conditions

On fur farms, animals are imprisoned in tiny wire-mesh cages for their entire lives until they are killed. For species such as mink and fox, these conditions are especially appalling, as they are wild animals and would naturally travel many miles each day. Being caged in huge sheds, where thousands of other animals are also imprisoned, drives them insane with anxiety and fear. Repetitive movements, such as head-bobbing and circling, are therefore common.

Methods of killing

Animals on fur farms are killed by electrocution (through the use of electrodes in the mouth and anus), gassing, lethal injection or neck breaking. These crude methods are employed to ensure that the pelts (the animals' skins and fur) are not damaged.

Fur trapping

The most commonly-used trap is the barbaric steel-jawed leghold trap. When set by the trapper, the spring-loaded jaws are opened to their fullest extent and secured with a metal clip. When an animal steps on it, the clip is released and the device snaps shut with incredible force. The intention is to catch the animal's leg, but they can also be caught across their back, neck or head. The trapped animal will be in agony, unable to escape, for hours or even days, until the trapper comes back to suffocate or beat them to death. Leghold traps do not discriminate. They catch any animal who treads on them. Trappers call these non-target animals 'trash'. The contraptions are now banned in 88 countries, including the UK, and in several states across the USA. However, fur is still imported to the UK from animals who have been killed by leghold traps in other countries.

Fur trade arguments

Supporters of the fur industry often claim that trapping is a tool of wildlife management and conservation. This is untrue. Many species of wild cats such as ocelots, margays, lynx and Geoffrey's cat are being driven to the verge of extinction by hunting and trapping. There are only 4,000-7,000 snow leopards left in the world. Sea otters were driven to the very edge of extinction and, despite protection, their numbers remain very low. The sea mink paid the ultimate price for having a beautiful fur coat – extinction.

Fur farmers try to insist that the animals are looked after very well and that they do not suffer when they are killed. Yet undercover footage shows time and again that the animals are going insane from their confinement, endlessly weaving and pacing in their desperation to be free. When they are killed, it often takes a few attempts to break the animals' necks, as they try to squirm their way out of their executioner's grip; or, if they are electrocuted, the terror as the electrodes are shoved into their mouth and anus is clear. When they cry out and their bodies convulse, there can be no doubt that these animals are dying in agony.

⇨ The above information is reprinted with kind permission from Animal Aid. Visit www.animalaid.org.uk for more information.

© Animal Aid

What you can do

⇨ Boycott shops selling fur. Write to, or email, the manager explaining the reason for your action – and let Animal Aid know about it so that we can send out an action alert for other people to do the same.
⇨ Do not buy clothes, toys, gloves, etc. with fur trim.
⇨ Write to your MEP (Member of the European Parliament) asking him or her to support a ban on the import of all fur – including cat and dog fur – and a ban on fur farming in Europe.
⇨ Join Animal Aid's youth group, Youth4Animals, and help campaign against the fur trade.

Fur fast facts

Information from the International Fur Trade Federation

Fur is a natural product, based on the sustainable use of renewable resources.

Fur farming

⇨ Is well regulated under international, national or regional laws and guidelines.

⇨ Is an established, natural part of the agricultural sector in many countries.

⇨ Provides high standards of care for animal health and animal welfare.

⇨ Is a valuable link in the food and recycling chain.

⇨ Provides an efficient use of 647,000 tonnes of animal by-products each year from the fishing and meat industries in the EU alone.

⇨ Provides manure for organic fertiliser.

⇨ Mink provides fat for hypoallergenic soaps and hair products.

Wild fur

⇨ Represents about 15% of the world's trade in fur.

⇨ National and international regulations ensure that only nature's surplus enters the fur trade each year.

⇨ No endangered species are used.

⇨ An International Agreement (the Agreement on International Humane Trapping Standards or AIHTS) has been signed by the main producers of wild fur; Canada, the EU and Russia to ensure that only the most humane techniques for trapping are used, based on veterinary research. The US has a similar agreement.

Economics

⇨ In 2007 the worldwide fur trade turned over US $billion 15,022.

⇨ The fur trade comprises hunting communities and many small farms and family businesses, craftsmen and women, manufacturers, dressing companies, co-operatively owned or publicly floated auction houses, designers and retailers. It is a small but global industry.

⇨ In Denmark, fur farming was worth Euro 514 million in 2002, the country's third largest export after bacon and cheese.

⇨ In Finland, the annual fur production value is Euro 250 million, greater than that of beef, with over 50% of fur farmers relying on fur farming as their sole source of income.

⇨ In Canada, the fur trade contributes Can$ 800 million to the Canadian economy, employing over 75,000 Canadians in total.

⇨ Hong Kong is the world's largest importer of farmed fur skins and remains the leading exporter of fur garments to the value of more than US$ 320 million annually.

⇨ In Russia, the value of the fur trade is over US$ 2.5 billion, contributing around 0.6% – 0.8% of the turnover of all consumer goods.

⇨ In the UK, fur brokers are responsible for buying the majority of the world's fur traded at raw or wholesale level, with a turnover of some US$ 750 million per annum.

Animal welfare and conservation

⇨ Over the last 20 years, the IFTF alone has contributed more than US$ 5 million in support of a wide range of animal welfare and conservation projects.

⇨ The IFTF has been a voting member of the IUCN (World Conservation Union) since 1985.

⇨ The European fur sector and national governments spent over Euro 1.6 million in 1999 on fur farming research.

⇨ European fur farmers helped to establish the Fur Animal Welfare Research Committee (FAWRC) in 1999, which reports to the Council of Europe's Standing Committee on farm animal welfare.

⇨ The European Fur Breeders' Association (EFBA) has its own Code of Practice, which incorporates the Council of Europe recommendations, with its own further 'best practice'.

⇨ North American fur breeders have Codes of Practice that include recommended methods of care from birth to death of mink and foxes.

⇨ In 2006 the IFTF and its Members introduced the independently monitored Origin Assured™ (OA™) Label to assure consumers that the fur garment comes 100% from a country with national or federal welfare regulations or standards in force. The IFTF also actively promotes accurate species labelling in fur products.

⇨ The international fur trade has implemented a voluntary ban on the trade in cat and dog skins since 2002, well ahead of the EU regulation to ban trade in domestic cat and dog skins, implemented in January 2009.

⇨ The above information is reprinted with kind permission from the International Fur Trade Federation. Visit www.iftf.com or www.furtrail.co.uk for more information on fur production.

© International Fur Trade Federation

Fur goodness sake: skinned alive for the catwalk

By Merrilees Parker

Three years ago, I was being fitted for my wedding dress when the designer suddenly produced a white fox-fur stole out of nowhere and draped it around my shoulders as a dramatic finishing touch.

I have always thought that fur is beautiful, but even then I had qualms about the ethics of wearing it and wondered where it had come from.

'Oh, it was probably a wild fox,' said the designer casually.

There was something undeniably indulgent and luxurious about wearing that fur on my wedding day, and whenever I looked at it in my wardrobe afterwards, I felt a certain guilt, given the care I take in sourcing my produce in my work as a chef.

Recently, however, I had an experience which made me feel physically sick every time I saw or touched it.

That experience was making a documentary for Channel 4 about the fur trade – an extraordinary venture which would see me gaining unprecedented access to a fur farm, take me animal trapping in the American wilderness and subject me to images of suffering which changed my views on wearing fur for ever.

I was first approached about this programme following an earlier documentary I had made for the BBC about chicken farming.

As a chef, I am careful to use only free-range meat, but I understand that single mums with four kids to feed need a cheaper alternative to the expensive organic and free-range options.

My argument was that there should be a middle ground – various other welfare improvements which would improve a chicken's lot without making it prohibitively expensive – and it was with the same open mind that I approached my investigation into the booming fur trade.

Fur is in the middle of a comeback – on the catwalks, in magazines and on the High Street.

Today, around 400 designers use fur, compared with only 45 in 1985, and the fur industry is worth £500 million a year in Britain alone – and a staggering £7 billion worldwide.

As I discovered for myself, fur no longer has the same shock value it did 20 years ago, when you risked verbal abuse and even physical attack if you dared wear it in public.

As an experiment, I was lent a full-length mink coat to wear when we began filming.

Nervously venturing out on to the streets of London, I was surprised to find that it didn't attract a single negative reaction – even when I stopped people and told them what I was wearing.

This change in attitude is perhaps not surprising given the endorsement of many celebrities who wear fur openly and with pride.

Given this new acceptance, and the sheer scale of the industry, there seems little point in hoping it will go away, so I wondered if there were ways of making fur more ethical.

Anti-fur campaigners have long condemned the industry as barbaric and inhumane, but surely, I thought, there must be good practices as well as bad.

If we could encourage the former, and warn consumers against the latter, then perhaps we could take some of the guilt out of wearing fur.

And in theory, why should the wearing of humanely sourced fur – from a regulated industry – be any different from wearing clothes made out of leather?

I had hoped the British fashion industry might co-operate, but I was to be disappointed.

I asked more than 100 British designers to talk on camera about their use of fur, but all declined, such was their fear of reprisals from the anti-fur lobby.

To get the industry's side of the story, I had to travel to Denmark where the Scandinavian fur industry has been busy courting designers by sponsoring their collections and encouraging them to work with fur.

This intensive drive to get their products into shops led me to hope that I might persuade at least one company to show me how animals live and die on a fur farm.

After intense negotiations, and with two PR minders watching our every move, we were allowed to film – for the first time – a farm where 20,000 mink every year are killed for their pelts.

It all seemed surprisingly humane, the mink raised in cages which were small but gave them at least some room to move around in before they were gassed with carbon dioxide.

I had expected lots of blood and screaming, but it all felt quite clean and clinical and no part of the animal was wasted.

As someone who works solely with free-range meat, I would never wear fur from mink farmed in this way, but, if you are comfortable with the general idea of wild creatures being kept in cages, then this Hilton of mink farms might well persuade you that mink farming is not as bad as the anti-fur campaigners claim.

The one doubt I had was whether this was all just a public relations exercise.

If fur farming can be that humane, why has it been outlawed in the UK?

For a different view, I visited the Nottingham offices of Respect For Animals, a lobby group that wields significant political clout and was instrumental in bringing about a ban on fur farming here.

Its director, Mark Glover, told me that I had indeed seen a highly sanitised version of fur farming and showed me videos shot by undercover campaigners which, he assured me, were far closer to the truth.

The first of these was filmed in a fox farm in America.

I watched horrified as I saw clearly distressed animals in cramped cages, chasing their tails psychotically in never-ending circles.

I covered my eyes as the camera cut to one fox sitting and trembling in its cage – its right leg stripped of its flesh and gnawed to the bone by the other crazed creatures around it.

As Glover explained, the fox furs harvested from these creatures are worth around only £30, so the farmers do not waste money on calling out vets, even when the foxes are in such obvious distress.

It was hard to believe that this footage was shot in the US, which argues that its industry is very well regulated, but far worse was to come in footage from China, which supplies half of all the world's fur.

This was also shot at a fox farm and I watched horrified as these animals were clubbed, stamped on, or dashed against the ground to subdue them.

Then, through my tears, I saw these poor creatures being literally skinned alive.

Afterwards, I found it difficult to erase these awful images from my mind, but still I wondered whether I might find a way to wear fur without a guilty conscience.

Could animals spend their time in the wild and then be killed humanely?

To find out, I went on a remarkable journey to Idaho, where I was taught to lay an animal trap by Vietnam veteran Johnnie Wisenhurst, who makes his living selling beaver pelts to local dealers for up to £150 a time, as six generations of his family have done before him.

From his point of view, he is trapping animals from a sustainable and perceived pest population.

Like the rest of the fur trade, trapping is controversial.

Animals have been known to chew their limbs off to escape, so, after setting our trap late one night, I was relieved to find the next morning that it had captured a beaver and killed it outright with no sign of a struggle.

In Idaho, trapping is open to anyone – a child as young as 12 can get a licence.

There are good trappers and bad ones.

Johnnie seemed to me to be one of the good guys, taking care not to cause unnecessary suffering to the animals he killed.

The problem for those who buy the myriad furs on the market today is that they have no way of knowing whether they were killed humanely, and the industry itself makes little or no effort to provide such information.

Some furs are 'Origin Assured', which means they come from a regulated country, but regulations vary from country to country and welfare standards can differ dramatically from farm to farm.

One auction house I visited in Denmark handles a third of the world's furs and sorts them not by country of origin, but by colour and quality.

One batch of 2,000 mink furs might contain furs from hundreds of suppliers from all over the world – some maintaining high standards of care, some not.

Even the buyers who bid for them do so without any knowledge of their provenance, so what hope does the consumer have of making an ethical choice when it comes to fur?

If they did have more information, would they care?

Unlike the food industry, where growing public concern has brought about improvements in animal welfare and transparency in labelling products, the people who wear fur don't seem to give a damn about how it has been produced.

Without pressure from its customers, the fur industry will remain unregulated and, as long as that is the case, anyone buying fur could be supporting animal cruelty. Is any item of clothing really worth that?

For me, the answer is an emphatic no.

After I had finished filming the documentary, one of the first things I did was cut up the fox stole I had worn at my wedding and throw it away.

Kill It, Skin It, Wear It aired on Channel 4, 10 August 2008 at 10pm.

⇨ This article first appeared in the *Daily Mail*, 9 August 2008.

Know the facts about fur

Get the facts and figures on this cruel trade...

⇨ Due to the ethical and moral reasons and based on animal welfare concerns, fur farming was banned in the UK from 2001.

⇨ In the EU, fur farming is banned in the UK, Netherlands (foxes only), Austria and Lander in Germany.

⇨ Mink farming is not banned in Ireland.

⇨ The worldwide fur industry killed more than 55 million animals in 2005 for their fur.

Recent polling by the RSPCA revealed that:*

⇨ 93 per cent of respondents would not wear real fur.

⇨ 92 per cent of respondents think that real or fake fur items should be clearly labelled according to the method of production.

⇨ 91 per cent would not consider buying a product that contains real fur even if it is available very cheaply.

⇨ 61 per cent thought there was a moral difference between farming animals that are farmed for meat and those that are farmed for fur.

⇨ 61 per cent said they do not think celebrities should wear real fur.

*TNS Omnibus survey on behalf of the RSPCA between 26th January and 4th February 2007

⇨ The above information is reprinted with kind permission from the RSPCA. Visit www.rspca.org.uk/fur for more information.

© RSPCA

UK circus animals given sufficient care, says report

Nelly the elephant unpacked her trunk and decided to stay at the circus after all

⇨ *Study finds animals kept in adequate conditions.*
⇨ *RSPCA criticises scope of government-backed report.*

**By James Randerson,
Science Correspondent**

Sinbad and Zebedee will be pounding the sawdust under their big top for a while longer thanks to a government-backed report which concluded there was no evidence that circus animals were kept in worse conditions than animals in other captive environments.

The result will delight the four British circuses out of 27 that still use animals in their acts – including Circus Mondao, which keeps the two performing zebras. But ministers at the Department for Environment, Food and Rural Affairs are left with an awkward decision on whether to ban wild animals in circuses after the report they commissioned into the science of animal welfare gave little to go on.

Animal circuses are much less common in Britain than in Europe. Although it is possible to watch acts including crocodiles, lions, snakes and even a kangaroo, the report estimates just 47 animals work regularly in circus rings in this country.

The circus community argues that animal shows are an important part of our cultural heritage, that the animals only perform natural behaviours and are kept to the best possible welfare standards.

Animal rights organisations argue that subjecting animals to training and transport between venues for entertainment is unethical. They are furious the working group which produced the report was given a restricted remit to look only at transportation and housing needs of non-domesticated species and not training.

On this question the report concludes there is not enough good scientific evidence to make the case either way.

'For the status quo to be changed the balance of evidence would have to present a convincing and coherent argument for change,' the working group's academic panel of six animal welfare experts wrote. 'Such an argument, based on a sound scientific basis, has not been made ... There appears to be little evidence to demonstrate that the welfare of animals kept in travelling circuses is any better or worse than that of animals kept in other captive environments.'

Animal rights campaigners were dismayed at the judgement. 'We didn't need a report telling us something that we already knew, which is the lack of peer-reviewed studies on the treatment of circus animals,' said a spokeswoman for the RSPCA. She said that although there were few studies on exotic species, studies of the transportation of other species such as farm animals could be applied.

Those on the industry side say the report negates what they regard as a prolonged campaign of smears linking circuses with cruelty. 'The animal

rights people have made that word circus so dirty,' said Petra Jackson, ringmistress at Circus Mondao. 'People have got to open their eyes and see what circus is about now and not

Roll up, roll up Britain's big top animals

The Great British Circus
⇨ 1 kangaroo
⇨ 2 llamas
⇨ 4 reindeer
⇨ 5 lions
⇨ 7 tigers
⇨ 7 camels
⇨ 1 zebra

Bobby Roberts Super Circus
⇨ 1 elephant (touring but retired from performance)
⇨ 1 camel

Circus Mondao
⇨ 3 zebras
⇨ 2 llamas
⇨ 2 camels

Jolly's Circus
⇨ 2 crocodiles
⇨ 1 zebra
⇨ 1 ankole (a form of African cattle)
⇨ 1 llama
⇨ 6 snakes

Animal cruelty? No
But I know where
I'd rather be if I had
a choice...

what it was about 30 years ago. I really do think it is snobbery. You can go to a county show and see people doing dog agility, but when you see people doing dog agility in a circus it all of a sudden becomes wrong.'

Chris Barltropp of the union Equity was chairman of the industry subcommittee which contributed to the report. 'It does seem that the circus community has been vindicated by this report. At last we have reached a point where we can set aside the name calling which has been going on for years from the animal rights organisations,' he said.

The report leaves ministers in a tricky position. Many MPs and peers are in favour of a ban. In March 2006 Ben Bradshaw, a Defra minister, said in parliament: 'I sympathise with the view that performances by some wild animals in travelling circuses are not compatible with meeting welfare needs.' He said the government wanted to introduce regulations under the Animal Welfare Act rather than through primary legislation, but the author of the current report believes that will not be possible.

Just 47 animals work regularly in circus rings in this country

Mike Radford, an expert on the legal aspects of animal welfare at Aberdeen University, said: '[Ministers] gave commitments in parliament that a ban would be based on scientific evidence and as yet there isn't any.'

Responding to the report, the environment secretary, Hilary Benn, said: 'The government will now want to hear reactions ... and consider its position.'

An Ipsos MORI opinion poll in October 2005 for Animal Defenders International found that 80% of people agree that the use of wild animals in circuses should be banned – 65% thought that all performing animals should be banned.

The RSPCA are currently running a campaign about circuses – please visit www.rspca.org.uk/circuses to find out more.
21 November 2007
© *Guardian Newspapers Limited 2008*

The cost of cheap meat

Cheap meat comes at a high price to animal welfare

Animals such as cattle, sheep, pigs, goats and horses are routinely transported across continents to satisfy an ever-increasing global demand for meat. To make this as cheap as possible, animals are transported in huge numbers resulting in enormous cruelty and suffering.

The main problems with live animal transport:
⇨ Overcrowding – Animals are crammed into vehicles and often get injured or may even be trampled to death.
⇨ Exhaustion and dehydration – They can be in transit for days, suffering extremes of temperature and often without sufficient food, water or rest. Many die as a result.
⇨ Animals are sentient beings – They feel pain and stress just like us.

When things go wrong

In addition to this routine suffering, often things go wrong with disastrous consequences for the animals. In 2003 the Cormo Express carried 57,000 sheep from Australia to Saudi Arabia but was not allowed to unload. The sheep remained on board for 3 months in appalling and deteriorating conditions. Over 5,000 died.

Compassion in World Farming believes that no animal should travel more than 8 hours to its final destination. It is widely accepted that animals should be fattened and slaughtered as near as possible to home. We believe that the transport of live animals should be replaced by a trade in meat.

The end of the road

The suffering often does not end when the journey is over. In many countries, animals are brutally loaded and unloaded using electric goads and sticks. Standards of slaughter vary enormously too. Some animals are inadequately stunned or not stunned at all before slaughter.

The spread of disease is another issue associated with the long-distance transport of live animals.

⇨ The above information is reprinted with kind permission from Compassion in World Farming. Visit www.ciwf.org.uk for more information.

© *Compassion in World Farming*

It may be cruel, but intensive farming saves lives

It's easy for some of us to buy free-range, but the lauding of farmers' markets ignores those for whom cheap food is essential

By Jay Rayner

A couple of years ago, during the recording of a food quiz on Radio 4, I listened to food writer and TV personality Hugh Fearnley-Whittingstall declare that he thought nobody should eat meat unless it had been reared in a completely free-range manner. One of the other contestants – Stephen Fry, as it happens – pointed out that free-range meat is very expensive and that not everybody could afford it.

'Well,' Fearnley-Whittingstall said confidently, 'there are always the cheaper cuts.' I was appalled and immediately reminded of the great line attributed to Marie Antoinette. For 'let them eat cake', read 'let them eat braising steak'.

I recalled the exchange last week while watching *Hugh's Chicken Run*, Fearnley-Whittingstall's series of campaigning programmes on Channel 4, arguing against the intensive, indoor rearing of chickens which provides 95 per cent of the birds we eat in this country and in favour of free-range methods.

It was engaging and emotive stuff, which is only to be expected. Fearnley-Whittingstall is an exceptionally clever and passionate communicator, who knows what makes for good television. The intensive rearing of chickens is an ugly business and by setting up his own poultry shed, complete with 17 birds per square metre, he brought the reality of that right into our sitting rooms.

It also made sense that he should be the one to do it. He has come to epitomise the obsessions at the very heart of Britain's vibrant middle-class, foodie culture. Fearnley-Whittingstall is an articulate champion of the virtues of seasonal and local food and argues convincingly that we need to understand exactly where the food we eat comes from. Indeed, his message is so sharp and focused that he has turned himself, and his River Cottage HQ in Dorset, into one of the most robust and profitable brands in Britain's media food world.

In an ideal world, we would all eat locally-sourced meat raised in the most glorious of conditions

And that's the problem. Because if his series, and pronouncements by others including Jamie Oliver, has proved anything, it is that somewhere along the line we have got our wires firmly crossed. We have managed to confuse our foodie obsessions – a set of lifestyle choices for the affluent – with a wider and much more serious debate on public nutrition that affects the very poorest in society. Let's agree that the worst excesses of intensive poultry rearing are deplorable and welcome the government's announcement last week that Britain would be following the rest of Europe by banning battery chicken egg production by 2012. That's good news. But the arguments against intensive poultry farming made by Fearnley-Whittingstall in his TV shows are nowhere near as straightforward as he tried to suggest.

Time and again during last week's programme, the issue of price was raised and the best he could do was argue that the difference – £6 for the free-range bird against £3 for the intensively reared – really wasn't that great. It was left to a marvellously stroppy single mother called Hayley from the housing estate in his local market town of Axminster to give him a reality check. 'You can afford to eat free-range,' she said. 'I can't.'

There was something uncomfortable about watching Fearnley-Whittingstall, a gentleman farmer, trying to guilt-trip people on low incomes over what they eat. There's no doubting his commitment. And yes, in an ideal world, we would all eat locally sourced meat raised in

the most glorious of conditions. Millions of people with the available cash spend their extra money to ensure they do just that. I am one of them. I am willing to spend a significant proportion of my income on ingredients, because I am a greedy man who has the luxury of being able to support an overly developed interest in his dinner.

But there are much bigger issues at play here and to understand them we need to take the long view. The reality is that the downside to human health from the factory farming of chicken – a certain amount of salmonella and campylobacter, both of which can be eliminated by proper handling in the kitchen – are vastly outweighed by the upside. However much the animal welfare lobby may disagree, it is arguable that the upside also outweighs the significant negatives for those intensively reared chickens.

'Prior to the 1950s, large numbers of people died because of tuberculosis due to a simple lack of nourishment,' says Hugh Pennington, emeritus professor of bacteriology at Aberdeen University and an expert on food contamination and nutritional issues. 'The wide availability of cheap animal proteins, both chicken and fish, has put an end to that.' The availability of those intensively reared chickens that go from egg to slaughter in just 39 days without ever seeing daylight is, therefore, not merely a question of taste to be pursued doggedly by a lovable TV chef. It's a question of basic human health.

To the growing battalions of Britain's foodies, this is nothing short of heresy. They decry the power of the supermarkets and rage against the industrialisation of food production in Britain, arguing instead for the value of independent shopkeepers, farmers' markets and the producers who supply them.

But trying to have a debate about public nutrition in Britain by pointing out the virtues of these admittedly wonderful ingredients is a little like trying to have a debate about public transport by pointing out the virtues of the Mercedes Five Series. The two are not related. The truth is that we live on a small, overpopulated island and if we are going to feed

ourselves – and, in particular, those who struggle with the weekly budget – we are going to have to face up to what that really means, which is the unglamorous, unsexy business of mass food production.

Fearnley-Whittingstall and campaigners like him argue that we have become too used to paying too little for what we eat. It takes less and less of the working week to earn the money necessary to pay for the weekly shop (if longer for some than others).

However that is changing. Food prices are being squeezed by a combination of a ravenously booming China, which is vacuuming up food supplies from across the world at a truly astonishing rate and a re-engineering of arable farming in the US where acre after acre of land is being given over to crops for biofuels rather than for human consumption. The price rises we have seen so far are as nothing against those to come.

To add to that by saying that intensive rearing of chicken should be abolished in favour of a free-range system is not only unrealistic but, for

families on low incomes, dangerous. Far more important than how the chicken is raised is the simple question of whether it ends up in the deep-fat fryer at the end. That is where the real issue in how we eat lies in this country.

Fearnley-Whittingstall will doubtless argue that all this is missing the point, that his campaign is actually about animal welfare. No surprise there. Sentimentality always has been the British vice, be it over children, our history or the saintly chicken. But like a wonderful, organically reared poulet de bresse, sentimentality is not something everybody can afford. You may be able to. But for a large number of people, people who do not have the luxury of being able to engage with the vivid, middle-class foodie culture encouraged by Jamie, Gordon and Hugh, it is too high a price to pay.

Jay Rayner is The Observer's restaurant critic and food writer
⇨ This article first appeared in *The Observer*, 13 January 2008.

The five freedoms

Information from the Farm Animal Welfare Council

A set of core husbandry principles, called the 'Five Freedoms', has been developed based on the level of suffering, pain, disease, discomfort, hunger, thirst, fear and distress endured by animals on farms and on their need to be able to engage in natural behaviour.

The 'Five Freedoms' are widely recognised by scientists and policy makers as a helpful way of assessing the strengths and weaknesses of animal husbandry practices.

1 Freedom from Hunger and Thirst – by ready access to fresh water and a diet to maintain full health and vigour.
2 Freedom from Discomfort – by providing an appropriate environment including shelter and a comfortable resting area.
3 Freedom from Pain, Injury or Disease – by prevention or rapid diagnosis and treatment.
4 Freedom to Express Normal Behaviour – by providing sufficient space, proper facilities and company of the animal's own kind.
5 Freedom from Fear and Distress – by ensuring conditions and treatment which avoid mental suffering.

⇨ The above information is reprinted with kind permission from the Farm Animal Welfare Council. Visit www.fawc.org.uk for more information.

Welfare issues for meat chickens

Information from Compassion in World Farming

Around 70% of chickens raised for meat globally are raised in intensive industrial farming systems. This includes the majority of chickens in the UK, Europe and the US as well as rapidly increasing numbers in developing countries.

Intensively farmed chickens are bred to reach their slaughter weight in less than 6 weeks. This is half the time it would take traditionally. Their short lives are spent in overcrowded sheds with no access to the outside.

> **Intensively farmed chickens are bred to reach their slaughter weight in less than 6 weeks**

Inside the intensive chicken shed

Broiler sheds are generally bare except for water and food points, with no natural light. There is litter on the floor to absorb droppings which is not usually cleared until the chickens are gathered for slaughter.

The air can become highly polluted with ammonia from the droppings. This can damage the chickens' eyes and respiratory systems and can cause painful burns on their legs (called hock burns) and feet.

It can get very hot inside the sheds, especially in summer. If the ventilation system fails, thousands of birds can die of heat stress.

Fast growth

Because they cannot move easily, the chickens are not able to adjust their environment to avoid heat, cold or dirt as they would in natural conditions.

The added weight and over-crowding also puts a strain on their hearts and lungs. In the UK alone, up to 19 million chickens die in their sheds from heart failure each year. Across the EU, this figure could be as much as 121 million.

Overcrowding

Tens of thousands of birds can be housed in each shed. The 2007 EU Directive allows the equivalent of 19 birds per square metre. This means that each bird has less floor space than the size of an A4 sheet of paper.

Chickens in overcrowded sheds lack exercise, are disturbed or trodden on when they are resting, have less and less space to move as they grow larger and may find it more difficult to reach food and drink if they are lame. They are unable to forage as they would naturally. Crowding is also likely to lead to more air pollution, increased heat stress and foul litter.

Feed restriction of breeders

Some chickens are allowed to live until sexual maturity in order to breed. Their food intake is often severely restricted otherwise their fast growth would damage their health. These chickens can be stressed, frustrated and chronically hungry as a result.

Catching, transport and slaughter

Before transport to slaughter, broilers are usually deprived of food for many hours. Catching, crating and transport are stressful and can result in bruising and other injuries. Around 20 million chickens per year are already dead by the time they arrive at EU slaughterhouses.

At the slaughterhouse, chickens are typically hung by their feet on shackles whilst conscious, which is likely to be painful, particularly as leg problems are common. The birds are usually stunned by being dipped, head first, into an electrified water bath before their throats are cut. This stunning is often ineffective: the struggling birds sometimes raise their heads and miss the water, resulting in fully conscious birds having their throats cut.

There are more humane alternatives to intensive chicken farming.

⇨ The above information is reprinted with kind permission from Compassion in World Farming. Visit www.ciwf.org.uk for more.

© Compassion in World Farming

Animal experiments

Q & A from the AMRC, a supporter of animal research in medicine

Why are animal experiments part of medical research?

The complexity and effects of disease cannot be imitated in a test-tube. Scientists use animals so that they can understand more about how disease processes affect the whole, living, body. It is also essential that new therapies are tested in this dynamic environment, rather than only in the artificial conditions provided by a test-tube or computer screen. For example, in a test-tube, it is impossible to see how cancer cells spread around the body or check whether medicine can get to the unhealthy tissue that needs it. Most people believe that it would be unethical to experiment on humans, which is why animals, as well as other systems such as cell cultures and computer simulations, are used in medical research. By law, animals cannot be used in research if there is an equally good non-animal alternative.

Which animals are used in medical research experiments?

The majority of animals used for medical research are rodents and all are bred especially for research. Of all the animals used, 84% (roughly eight out of ten) are mice or rats, 12% are fish, amphibians or birds, 2.1% are sheep, cows or pigs, 1.5% are rabbits or ferrets and 0.3% are dogs and cats. A very small fraction, less than a sixth of 1%, are monkey (primate) species. In the UK it is illegal to use chimpanzees, orang-utans or gorillas. In fact, the UK has the strictest rules in the world governing animal research and this ensures that animals are only used when absolutely essential. All animal use is regulated by the Home Office through the Animals (Scientific Procedures) Act (1986).

It is important to remember that animals benefit from this research too. Around half of the medicines originally developed for use in humans are also used to treat ill animals, and some scientists use animal experiments to investigate diseases that only affect animals.

Which animal species are protected by law?

All living vertebrates, i.e. animals that have a backbone, and the common Octopus (*Octopus vulgaris*) are protected under the Animals (Scientific Procedures) Act (1986). This includes immature mammals, birds and reptiles from halfway through gestation or incubation, plus fish and amphibians that are capable of independent feeding. The Home Office runs the regulatory system. Under the Act, every research project must be assessed to ensure that the use of animals is justified and that their suffering is kept to a minimum.

Why can't scientists use humans instead of animals?

Animals are small, they reproduce quickly and it is possible to study disease development over a much shorter time period than would ever be possible using a human; a mouse has a life span of only a few years. In addition, researchers often need to be able to look at tissue once the experiment is finished, which could not be achieved if a living human were used. Animals can also be genetically modified in ways which make them better models for human disease.

Do the animals used in experiments suffer any pain?

It would be untrue to claim that animals never suffer during research, but this pain has to be considered in context. Most people would not take the view that four weeks of mild arthritis in a rat is the same as 20 years of crippling arthritis for your grandmother. Researchers recognise that animals do sometimes feel pain as a result of their experiments and must ensure that this is minimised as far as possible. Many experiments only cause momentary distress, for example taking a blood sample or giving medication, and using an anaesthetic during such procedures would cause an animal greater discomfort than not using it. It is also important to note that animal experimentation does not mean that pain is inevitable, for example, some experiments are based on painless procedures to observe behaviour.

All laboratory procedures that

PROTECTED UNDER THE ANIMAL (SCIENTIFIC PROCEDURES)ACT !

Think that will fool them?

involve animals require a licence. Methods of handling and performing procedures have been developed over many years and researchers work with the Home Office to ensure that suffering is kept to a minimum. In addition, a vet is employed at every facility where animals are used for research.

It is important to remember that all suffering is not necessarily related to pain. An animal may suffer because it is stressed by its surroundings, in the same way that a cancer patient may feel anxious in hospital. To ease stress in laboratory animals, they are fed and housed in ways that are right for them. In addition, the animals are put down humanely, which is not always the case in the wild. All decisions to use animals in research are based on the principles of the 3Rs: reduction, replacement and refinement. With regards to the latter, animal experiments are constantly being refined in order to reduce stress and pain. A good example of this is the use of fluorescence to visualise tumour growth in mice used for cancer research. The mouse can run around its cage as researchers observe tumour growth using the fluorescence, so the animal doesn't have to be put down to assess how much the tumour has grown. This example has the added benefit that the experiment can be completed before the mouse starts to show signs of distress.

The 2002 MORI poll on the use of animals in medical research found that, when suffering is kept to a minimum, 87% of the general public support animal use in research, and this rises to 90% for research into life-threatening disease. Less animal distress, including pain, is exactly what refinement aims to achieve, while reducing the numbers of animals used in research, and ultimately replacing them altogether, are also key aims.

Animals and humans are not identical so why use animals to study human disease?

A mouse and a human being both have a heart, lungs, kidneys, central nervous system, immune system, liver, bowel, stomach and other vital organs. In both species, these organs do the same jobs and so behave in similar ways; this makes the mouse a good model of a human. Researchers rarely use animals to mimic full-blown human disease, instead, they focus on just one stage or one tissue interaction to try to understand the disease more fully.

Though mice and people certainly don't look the same, we are genetically very similar: at least 80% of our DNA is identical. Even non-mammals, like the nematode worm (we share 35% of our genes), have provided information about cancer, helping us to better understand the disease and how to prevent and treat it.

⇨ The above information is re-printed with kind permission from the Association of Medical Research Charities. Visit www.amrc.org.uk for more information.
© Association of Medical Research Charities

What's wrong with animal experiments?

Information from the Dr Hadwen Trust

The Dr Hadwen Trust opposes animal experiments because of both ethical and scientific concerns. We believe it is unethical to subject animals in the laboratory to physical pain and suffering and mental distress. We also believe that animal research has significant scientific limitations because of the differences between humans and other animals.

The ethical case against animal experiments

Globally an estimated 115 million animals are used in laboratories each year. Cats, dogs, rabbits, mice and other animals, no different to those we love as pets, are used in laboratories. Monkeys are also used in their thousands.

In the name of research, animals can be force-fed harmful substances; infected with lethal viruses; subjected to brain damage, heart attacks, strokes and cancers and ultimately killed. It is clearly recognised in British and European Union law that animals used in experiments can experience 'pain, distress, suffering or lasting harm'.

The brain centres and circuits that underlie the unpleasant emotional aspects of pain, including fear, anxiety, memory and anticipation, are not unique to humans. Beyond physical pain, other animals also have thoughts, anxieties, intentions and memories. It is now well established in scientific literature that animals in laboratories can suffer mental distress from confinement, frustration, fear and isolation. The increases in stress hormones, ulcers, immune suppression, abnormal behaviour and brain dysfunction seen in laboratory animals demonstrates that they often suffer from the stress of coping with laboratory life itself.

Those who defend animal experiments do so on the basis that humans – all humans – are unique in a morally relevant way when compared to other animals. Of course, every species is unique in its complement of mental and physical abilities, but some of these are not morally relevant in this context. Animals don't need to be able to drive a car or vote in elections to suffer in experiments.

Promoting the 'uniqueness' of humanity compared to other animals also risks excluding some people from our sphere of moral concern. Those who argue that humans are morally different from all other animals by virtue of their higher cognitive functions, complex language skills or advanced mathematical abilities would, logically, have to exclude people in a persistent coma, and some people with dementia or brain damage, as well as infants. Following that rationale to its logical conclusion could lead to acceptance of forcible experimentation on some people, a concept we all abhor.

There is no morally relevant logical or biological distinction between all humans and all other animals. Therefore it follows that either invasive experiments on all sentient creatures – human and otherwise – are morally wrong; or that such experiments on animals and on some unconsenting people, are right.

Another common argument used to promote animal experiments states that research on animals is necessary for medical progress. However, if perceived necessity was considered sufficient justification for the infliction of pain and suffering in research and testing, over-riding ethical arguments, then forcible human experimentation would actually be acceptable and even scientifically preferable to using animals as surrogates for people. Regrettably, this has happened in several countries in the past.

The Dr Hadwen Trust takes the same ethical approach to experiments on animals as we do to experiments that would harm vulnerable, unconsenting humans: that is, such experiments are wrong in principle, whether or not others might hope to benefit.

The scientific case against animal experiments

In medical research and testing, animal experiments have serious scientific limitations which are of particular concern given the degree of confidence that is generally placed in them, often without proof of validity.

There are many species differences in anatomy (body structures), metabolism, physiology (systems functions) or pharmacology (cellular receptors, drug effects), between different animals, including humans. These differences are underlaid by genetic variations. Even subtle molecular differences can have a significant effect on the validity of results when 'translated' from animals to humans.

Laboratory animals almost never suffer naturally from human illnesses, but artificially inducing selected symptoms of human diseases in so-called animal 'models' seldom replicates the human disorders.

For example:
⇨ Stroke: blocking an artery to the brain of monkeys or rats does not replicate a human stroke. Decades of such research have produced more than 114 stroke drugs that worked in animals, but were not safe and effective in patients.
⇨ Parkinson's disease: monkeys are injected with a toxic chemical that induces a disorder superficially similar to human Parkinson's disease. However, the monkeys partly recover from the condition whereas Parkinson's disease in patients is irreversible and incurable.
⇨ Heart disease: dogs are widely used for research into heart disease, despite numerous differences between dog and human hearts, blood vessels and circulation. For example, high blood pressure in obese patients is associated with high insulin levels in the blood, yet in dogs high insulin levels actually lower blood pressure.
⇨ Septic shock: this is the leading cause of death in intensive care units and has been studied for decades in animals. Of numerous therapies found to improve survival in animals, none have worked in humans and even worse, some have decreased patients' survival.
⇨ AIDS: billions of pounds have been spent trying to create animal models of AIDS with little success. At least 50 animal-tested HIV vaccines have failed in human trials, and none have succeeded.

With animal experiments providing potentially misleading results, it is irresponsible to portray animal research as a 'gold standard' and all the more vital that we replace it with more humane and scientifically rigorous techniques.

We all want medical research to succeed in finding cures and treatments for human health problems. However, research on animals can produce conflicting or confusing results of unknown relevance to people and this can have serious implications, at worst misleading researchers about an illness and delaying medical progress.

Despite this, it is often claimed by those defending them, that medical progress is dependent on animal experiments. The truth is, animal experiments certainly have a long history of use, but that is not the same as established validity. There have only been a relatively small number of rigorous 'systematic reviews' of the validity of animal experiments. Most of those reviews have been critical either of the predictive accuracy for humans and/or of the quality and design of the animal studies. Find out more about systematic reviews.

A century or more ago, when medical research was asking simple questions about the basic circulation of the blood or the actions of hormones, using animals as surrogates would have been more scientifically advantageous (although no less unethical). But today the medical questions we need to answer are far more subtle. If a new drug depends for its safety and efficacy on stimulating, via a precise receptor mechanism, a chosen subset of immune cells in the bloodstream, then very minor species variations can spell disaster – as we saw with the TGN1412 clinical trial catastrophe in 2006, when six healthy volunteers nearly died despite the drug having been tested in monkeys and other animals.

For some diseases such as multiple sclerosis where little progress has been made in spite of decades of animal experiments, the conclusion must be that the animal models are failing to elucidate the human condition, and may well have actually obscured our understanding of it. By contrast, at the start of the 21st century, non-animal techniques have become the cutting edge of medical research, frequently proving cheaper, quicker and more effective.

⇨ The above information is re-printed with kind permission from the Dr Hadwen Trust. Visit www. drhadwentrust.org.uk for more information.

© Dr Hadwen Trust

Animal experiments – statistics

Statistics on the use of animals in scientific procedures in Great Britain

Statistics for 2007 – the main points

1 Just over 3.2 million scientific procedures were started in 2007, a rise of about 189,500 (6%) on 2006. The increased animal use was mainly due to increases in the use of mice, fish and domestic fowl, whilst the use of most other species was down when compared to 2006. The use of mice increased for fundamental research and breeding. There was increased use of fish in applied studies for human medicine and protection of man, animals and the environment. The use of domestic fowl increased for applied veterinary studies.

2 Mice, rats and other rodents were used in the majority of procedures; 83% of the total. Most of the remaining procedures used fish (10%), and birds (4%).

3 Dogs, cats, horses and non-human primates, afforded special protection by the Act, were collectively used in less than 1% of all procedures.

4 Approximately 4,000 procedures used non-human primates, down 240 (6%) from 2006, due to a decrease in both old-world and new-world species (for details on primate species, see appendix B available on RDS website).

5 Over a third of all procedures in 2007 were accounted for by breeding procedures (37%), for the production of harmful mutant and genetically modified animals. Mainly mice (93%) and fish (6%) were used in these procedures.

6 Around 99% of procedures carried out on animals listed in Schedule 2 of the Act used animals acquired from designated sources in the United Kingdom.

7 Genetically normal animals were used in 1.73 million regulated procedures (54% of all procedures), up 86,200 (5%) on 2006 figures. This increase is associated with mice used in fundamental studies and fish used in safety studies.

8 Species with harmful genetic mutations were used in 315,600 regulated procedures (10% of all procedures), down 11,000 (3%) from 2006. The majority of these procedures used rodents (91%); most of the remainder were fish or amphibians.

Mice, rats and other rodents were used in the majority of procedures; 83% of the total

---

9 Genetically modified animals were used in 1.15 million regulated procedures, up 114,400 (11%), representing thirty-six per cent of all procedures for 2007, compared with 34% in 2006 and 8% in 1995. The vast majority (99%) of these procedures used mice and fish.

10 Around 39% of all procedures used some form of anaesthesia to alleviate the severity of the interventions. For many of the remaining procedures the use of anaesthesia would have potentially increased the adverse effects of the procedure.

11 Non-toxicological procedures accounted for about 87% of the procedures started in 2007. This contrasts with 75% of such procedures in 1995. The main areas of use were for immunological studies, pharmaceutical research and development, cancer research, anatomy and physiology.

12 Procedures for toxicological purposes accounted for 13% of all procedures started in 2007. This contrasts with 25% of such pro-cedures in 1995. Since 1995 there has been a fall of 39%. In 2007 the majority (78%) of procedures were for pharmaceutical safety and efficacy evaluation. Around 78% of toxicological procedures in 2007 used rodent species, while non-human primates were used in less than 1%. Of all the toxicological procedures conducted in 2007, 87% were performed to conform to legal or regulatory requirements.

Statistics from previous years

The Home Secretary publishes statistics on the use of animals in scientific procedures in Great Britain annually, usually in July or August. Statistics for Northern Ireland are published separately.

Trends in animal use

There has been a significant reduction in the annual number of scientific procedures since 1976, this trend levelled out in the 1990s and in recent years there has been an increase in the number of procedures. Since 2000 the number of procedures has risen by 7%, with the rise in breeding procedures accounting for a significant part of this increase.

New molecular biology techniques are opening up new areas of research which will lead to an increase in the use of genetically modified animals. In addition, new regulatory proposals set out in the European Union Chemicals Strategy White Paper will, if agreed and implemented, also lead to increased use of animals for human health and safety purposes.

⇨ The above information is re-printed with kind permission from the Home Office. Visit http://scienceandresearch.homeoffice.gov.uk for more information.

© Crown copyright

Should we experiment on animals?

As a forthcoming European Union directive promises to transform the way testing on animals is carried out, a researcher and an animal advocate debate whether the practice can ever be justified

Should we experiment on animals? Yes, says Colin Blakemore

Antibiotics, insulin, vaccines for polio and cervical cancer, organ transplantation, HIV treatments, heart-bypass surgery – it reads like an A to Z of medical progress. But these major advances have something in common: they were all developed and tested using animals.

Animal experimentation is a contentious issue, but it boils down to two essential questions: does it work, and is it ethical?

The first is easy to answer: it works. Some would have you believe there are alternatives for all animal research, or that animal testing is always misleading and unsafe. These are fallacies.

Where there are reliable alternatives,

of course, we use them – that's what the law demands. Magnetic resonance imaging, computer models and work on isolated tissues and cell cultures can be useful; but they cannot provide the answers that animal research can.

No one chooses to use animals where there is no need. It gives no one any pleasure, and it is time-consuming, expensive and – quite rightly – subject to layers of regulation. Yet it is still the best way of finding out what causes disease, and of knowing whether new treatments will be safe and effective.

Biologically, we are similar to species such as mice and rats, because we have practically the same set of genes. Their bodies respond to disease and treatments much as ours do. If a genetically modified 'purple tomato' can fight cancer in mice, as announced yesterday, it might work for humans, too.

Medical research is an arduous process. By the time a therapy reaches the patient, it is easy to forget just how important animals were in its development. Patients might not know that the powerful new drugs Avastin (for bowel, breast and lung cancer) and Herceptin (for breast cancer) were developed after research on mice.

In fact, animal research has contributed to 70 per cent of Nobel prizes for physiology or medicine. Without it, we would – medically speaking – be stuck in the Dark Ages.

It is not only drugs and vaccines. Just last week, researchers in Seattle announced that they had used an electronic brain implant to enable a monkey to move its paralysed limbs, a discovery with the potential to allow severely disabled people to regain movement.

I challenge anyone who has followed the tragic case of Daniel

James, who committed suicide after becoming paralysed in a rugby accident, to try to stop research in the UK on spinal injuries, some of which involves rats.

Far from being ashamed of this kind of research, we should be proud of our scientists, whose work offers hope to those suffering from incurable disorders.

But what of the ethical issues? Some say that saving people from suffering is no excuse for the death of laboratory animals.

Those who object are entitled to refuse treatments that have been developed through animal tests – even if that means rejecting virtually every medical treatment that exists.

But they don't have the right to force that opinion on the majority, who expect and yearn for new and better treatments.

We all hope for a day when animal research is no longer needed, but until then it is vital. To curb animal research – including, in special cases, research on monkeys – would impede the flow of treatments to people who need them.

Medical researchers are not a bunch of scalpel-wielding lunatics. Those I know are compassionate, humane people who carry out their work with great caution and consideration, and with every effort to minimise suffering.

There are incurable diseases out there – for example Alzheimer's, multiple sclerosis and schizophrenia – that shatter lives. If we are to have any hope of treating such conditions, medical research needs every tool at its disposal. For everyone's sake, that must include animals.

Colin Blakemore is professor of neuroscience at Oxford and Warwick universities and former head of the Medical Research Council.

Should we experiment on animals? No, says Gill Langley

As scientists and human beings, we have a moral duty to prevent suffering wherever possible, whether in humans, mice or monkeys. But if you use animals in research or testing, pain and suffering are inevitable.

Yes, such experiments are regulated, but that regulation still permits animals to be infected with fatal diseases and to be lethally poisoned without pain relief. In British laboratories today, animals are still burned, paralysed, brain-damaged, and given heart attacks and electric shocks.

There is growing evidence that the value of animal experiments has often been overstated, and their limitations seriously underplayed. For far too long, animal scientists have avoided casting an essential critical eye over their work. But the evidence increasingly suggests that much medical progress has been made in spite of animal experiments, not because of them.

For example, last year the *British Medical Journal* published an independent review of treatments for five human illnesses, which found that drugs that worked in animals were useful for humans in only 50 per cent of cases. That's a success rate similar to tossing a coin.

Medical research based on such poor odds wastes animals' lives and must be delaying vital treatments. When that research involves the use of non-human primates, our close evolutionary cousins, it becomes even more contentious.

Some primate researchers say these experiments can't be replaced with non-animal research methods, a claim refuted in a new report by members of the Focus on Alternatives coalition. *Replacing Primates in Medical Research* looks at five key areas.

In each, there has been a catalogue of failed treatments. For example, at least 37 HIV vaccines that have been tested on primates have failed in humans; none has succeeded. In the case of stroke treatments, 95 experimental drugs have passed animal tests but failed in human clinical trials.

Developing more research techniques that don't involve animals is in all our interests. It offers an end to animal suffering, better research tools and improved therapies. Non-animal replacements have already led to advances in human medicine.

My charity, the Dr Hadwen Trust, funds the development of research techniques to replace animal experiments.

For example, our recent research at London's Institute of Cancer developed the world's first three-dimensional, multi-cellular test-tube model of early human breast cancer, to replace tests involving the implantation of tumours in mice.

Already, this research has revealed that certain cells in healthy breast tissue can suppress tumour growth, in a way that they cannot in cancerous tissue.

Safe, ethical studies of human patients are also substituting for animal experiments that many believed couldn't be replaced. Similarly, defenders of animal research claim that only animals can be used to study the effects of drugs on entire organs.

Yet we now have advanced computer simulations of human organs that allow 'virtual' experiments to predict how medicines will affect specific patient groups.

Then there is a new technique called RNA interference, which enables scientists to knock out selected genes in human cells instead of testing the techniques on animals.

Laboratories where medical progress is gained without pain and suffering are an entirely realistic goal – and the current revision of Europe's animal experiments legislation provides a vital opportunity to implement measures that could benefit animals and people alike. It's an opportunity that must not be wasted.

Dr Gill Langley is science director at the Dr Hadwen Trust for Humane Research (www.drhadwentrust.org)
10 November 2008
© Telegraph Group Limited, London 2008

Relevance of animal research

Information from the Association of Medical Research Charities

The leading medical research charities which are members of the Association of Medical Research Charities (AMRC) plan their research carefully to ensure that it is relevant, well thought-out and avoids duplication. They use expert panels to ensure they have the best advice on which research to fund – a process known as peer review – and then only fund research which involves animals when the research is really necessary and valuable.

Some antivivisectionists argue that animal experiments are useless because animals are different from humans. This is misleading for a number of reasons:

An animal's body is actually very similar to a human's. Even mice share around 98% of their genes with humans, and most of their basic chemistry is the same.

Animals share many diseases with humans, and research has helped animals too. More than half the drugs used by vets were developed for human medicine.

Each year, millions of people in this country benefit from treatments which have been developed in part through using animals. These annual figures speak for themselves:

⇨ 4,000 Artificial heart valves fitted.
⇨ 35,000 People treated for breast cancer.
⇨ 180,000 Diabetics using insulin.
⇨ 3,000,000 Operations under general or local anaesthetic.
⇨ 30,000,000 Prescriptions for asthma.
⇨ 50,000,000 Prescriptions for antibiotics.
Updated July 2008

⇨ The above information is reprinted with kind permission from the Association of Medical Research Charities. Visit www.amrc.org.uk for more information.

© AMRC

Research and testing using animals

Information from the Home Office

The development of drugs and medical technologies that help to reduce suffering among humans and animals depends on the carefully regulated use of animals for research.

The number of experiments involving live animals has halved in the last 30 years

We respect the fact that people have strong ethical objections to the use of animals in scientific procedures. We have legislated so experimentation is only permitted when there is no alternative research technique and the expected benefits outweigh any possible adverse effects.

Reducing research and testing using animals

The number of experiments involving live animals has halved in the last 30 years due to the:

⇨ development of new research techniques for example, a technique that enables testing of new drugs for fever-causing agents using human blood cells instead of rabbits;

⇨ introduction of rigorous standards stipulating that animal tests can't be conducted when there is a validated alternative research technique.

How we protect animal welfare

The breeding and supply of animals for use in scientific procedures is regulated in the UK by the Animals (Scientific Procedures) Act 1986.

Proposals to use animals in scientific projects are individually scrutinised. Project licences are only granted when:

⇨ there is no validated alternative to animal tests;

⇨ the generation of new test data is justified;

⇨ the protocols proposed cannot be further refined;

⇨ the protocols will be likely to produce data which will meet the specified objective.

All laboratories granted a licence must adhere to a strict code of practice which stipulates minimum standards for:

⇨ animal housing and environment;

⇨ animal care and health;

⇨ minimised breeding of surplus animals;

⇨ humane killing.

All licensed laboratories are closely monitored and our trained officers make unannounced inspections.

Oversight and advice

The Animals in Scientific Procedures (ASP) Inspectorate provides scientific advice to the Home Secretary and to officials who operate the system that approves licences for laboratories.

We've also established the Animal Procedures Committee (APC) to advise us on matters relating to any scientific procedures which may cause an animal pain, suffering, distress or lasting harm.

Tackling animal rights extremism

Animal rights extremists have conducted a sustained campaign of harassment and intimidation against the animal research industry, including targeting people at home and in their communities.

We are determined to stand up to animal rights extremism by:

⇨ ensuring that lawful and properly conducted research and business can take place freely in the UK by ending the threat of unlawful disruption and intimidation by animal rights extremists;

⇨ deterring and prosecuting animal rights extremists so that they no longer pose a threat from unlawful direct action.

⇨ The above information is reprinted with kind permission from the Home Office. Visit www.homeoffice.gov.uk for more information.

© Crown copyright

The three Rs

Information from the Research Defence Society

No one wants to use animals unnecessarily or to cause them unnecessary suffering. The guiding principles underpinning the humane use of sentient animals in scientific research are called the three Rs. Any researcher planning to use animals in their research must first show why there is no alternative and what will be done to minimise numbers and suffering, i.e.:

⇨ Replace the use of animals with alternative techniques, or avoid the use of animals altogether.

⇨ Reduce the number of animals used to a minimum, to obtain information from fewer animals or more information from the same number of animals.

⇨ Refine the way experiments are carried out, to make sure animals suffer as little as possible. This includes better housing, and improvements to procedures which minimise pain and suffering and/or improve animal welfare.

Replace

Non-animal techniques are often a spin-off from advances in science and technology. New approaches such as tissue engineering, stem cell technologies and computer modelling show promise for replacing animals in some areas of research. But many alternative methods, such as cell cultures, often give only very limited information about what happens in a whole living animal.

Effort devoted to replacing safety tests has produced some notable successes, particularly for assessing substances applied to the skin. Other new tests are being developed, but progress is limited and difficult. This is partly because regulatory authorities take a cautious approach to safety testing new medicines and other products.

Reduce

Considerable progress has been made in finding ways to reduce the numbers of animals used in experiments. Further reduction may come from more thorough analysis of the findings of studies already conducted (by 'systematic reviews') and by improving animal models for certain areas of research.

Proper experimental design and statistical analysis of the proposed research project allow the optimum number of animals to be used. If too few animals are used then the results are not reliable and the experiment needs to be repeated, using more animals. If too many animals are used, the results are reliable, but animal life has been wasted.

All other aspects of the experiment must be properly designed and conducted. Good experimental design will minimise variability and reduce bias. For example, selecting genetically identical animals makes it possible to get reliable answers using fewer animals. More consistent results can be achieved if the animals are born and bred in ultra-clean conditions and are free of infections or illnesses that might otherwise interfere with the study.

The development of other specific techniques can also reduce the number of animals required. A good example is modern imaging, whereby some effects of a treatment can be followed in individual animals in real time rather than by post-mortem examination of animals killed at different stages.

Refine

Refinement not only benefits animals, but can also improve the quality of research findings by reducing the level of stress in animals. By law, any suffering to an animal must be kept to a minimum. For example, anaesthetics are used for surgery, and painkillers are given as necessary afterwards. If animals have a painful or fatal disease, they can be humanely killed before they show severe symptoms.

Laboratory animals spend a lot of time in the animal house not being used in an experiment. Improving their living conditions is called environmental enrichment. Animals are normally kept in social groups, preferably in large cages or floor pens, with things for them to play with. Rabbits may get bedding material, boxes and tubes. Rodents like to have nesting material. Dogs like toys and a social environment. Monkeys like branches, swings, ropes and platforms. Their diet can also be made more interesting with fruit and other titbits, and foraging for it adds to their enjoyment.

Radio-operated devices can be implanted to measure blood pressure, heart rate and activity levels so that the animal does not have to be repeatedly caught and restrained. Using reward systems, animals can also be trained to co-operate, thereby reducing stress. For instance, monkeys can be taught to sit on weighing scales, or to hold out a limb so that a blood sample can be taken.

Combining the three Rs

In some cases it is possible to develop a whole new way of conducting a test involving fewer animals. For example, the LD50 test was used for many years to find out how toxic chemicals are. Scientists developed better tests, to do the same job but using fewer animals and designed so that none intentionally received a fatal dose. The LD50 is now banned in the UK. Moreover, a recent review conducted by the pharmaceutical industry showed that much of the data from single dose acute toxicity tests in rodents can be collected from other tests, meaning that fewer rodents are required in the development of new medicines.

⇨ The above information is re-printed with kind permission from the Research Defence Society. Visit www.rds-online.org.uk for more information.

© RDS

Animal testing – myths and reality

Information from the Association of the British Pharmaceutical Industry

Myth – Medicines don't need to be tested on animals

Reality - Medicines do need to be tested on animals to ensure that they are adequately safe to test on people. No regulatory authority would allow patients to take a medicine that hadn't first been tested on animals. The choice is a stark one: either we undertake animal research or we stop developing new medicines.

Myth – There are lots of ways to carry out these tests without using animals

Reality - At the moment, non-animal tests – such as those using cell cultures or computers – are limited because they don't reveal the full impact of a medicine on the major organs of the body.

Myth – Animals are nothing like humans – any information that you get from them is useless

Reality - There are great biological similarities between humans and animals. Of course there are some differences, but these will be taken into account during any trial. It's important to remember that animal research provides the information needed to ensure that a medicine is safe enough for humans to trial. It is a vital step in the development of new medicines.

Myth – Nobody knows what scientists get up to behind closed doors

Reality - Animal research is strictly monitored. Government inspectors can – and do – make regular spot checks to ensure that companies follow the regulations. The law states that animals should be well looked after and humanely treated.

Myth – More animals are used than is necessary

Reality - Pharmaceutical companies are constantly looking to reduce the number of animals used in tests. Whenever appropriate, non-animal methods such as laboratory simulations and tissue cultures are used. In addition, the Home Office regularly examines the number of animals used in research to ensure that only the minimum number of tests is undertaken.

Myth – If only companies shared their results, the number of animals used could be reduced

Reality - All medicines are unique and each one will have a different effect. Even medicines in the same class will show crucial differences. A small chemical change can have a significant impact on effectiveness and safety. It would be dangerous to make assumptions based on tests of similar, but not identical, compounds.

Myth – Animal research is cheap, so pharmaceutical companies use it to make bigger profits

Reality - Animal testing is neither cheap nor easy. Indeed, if the pharmaceutical industry was motivated by cost alone, it would not use animals at all.

Myth – Animal research gives misleading information, making medicines look safe when they are not. This is why medicines have unexpected side-effects

Reality - No one expects animal trials to tell researchers everything, but they do provide a good starting point. Animal research can indicate what reactions to expect in patients. It also provides information on dosages, ensuring that human studies can be conducted safely. It takes years to build up a clear picture of how a medicine works and behaves – animal research represents just one piece in the jigsaw.

⇨ The above information is reprinted with kind permission from the Association of the British Pharmaceutical Industry. Visit www. abpi.org.uk for more information.

© Association of the British Pharmaceutical Industry

Alternatives to animal experimentation

Alternatives reduce the number of animals used in a study, refine studies so the animals are subjected to a milder procedure or completely replace the need for animals

The latter – replacement – is clearly the most desirable but it is also difficult to achieve. Like all mammals, humans are very complicated and so are the diseases that beset them. At present, it is simply impossible, for example, to recreate the interplay of vital organs, the workings of the immune system, or the most likely toxic effects of a new medicine in non-animal experiments alone.

There is every incentive for scientists to use fewer animals in their research. This is not only for humane and legal reasons, but because animal research is expensive and time-consuming.

Alternatives are the law in Britain. The Government will not allow an animal experiment to go ahead if it can be done without animals. Also, each laboratory that carries out animal research has an ethical review process. Those involved will want to know what efforts have been made to find and use alternatives. So too will any organisation, such as a charity, that is funding the research. The funder's ethical review process includes checking that alternatives have been considered.

The description 'alternative' is sometimes used as shorthand for any non-animal method. Most medical research – over 90% in cost terms – does not use live animals at all. Computers, epidemiology, cells, tissues, imaging, high-throughput screening and clinical trials with people are common non-animal options. Animal research is one of a range of different methods available to scientists when it comes to understanding the mysteries of diseases and their treatment. These methods complement each other. While the non-animal approaches may not have been introduced specifically

to replace animal experiments, they often do have that benefit.

Computers are routinely used to study what is likely to happen when a living body breaks down a new medicine in the stomach or liver. The computer programs cannot reproduce every aspect but they can now be trusted to identify some of the factors that would cause a new medicine to fail in humans. In the past that would have required animals.

Alternatives are the law in Britain. The Government will not allow an animal experiment to go ahead if it can be done without animals

---

Artificial organs have been created, such as for the lung and intestine, that can also help discard candidate medicines that are unlikely to work in the way doctors would wish. As

with computers, these artificial organs cannot cover everything, and the chemicals that pass this stage will need to be tested on animals later, but they do reduce the overall numbers.

Alternatives that reduce, refine or replace (the 3Rs) are developed in a number of ways. There are organisations (such as FRAME) dedicated to finding new ones, while biomedical researchers and animal technicians themselves are responsible for many innovations. Modern information technology helps enormously here as electronic bulletins of what's new can be identified and distributed quickly.

All new alternatives face the challenge of being accepted by the scientific community and by those who regulate medical advances. They have to be validated to be sure they are a satisfactory replacement. This takes time.

⇨ The above information is reprinted with kind permission from the Coalition for Medical Progress. Visit www.medicalprogress.org for more information.

© Coalition for Medical Progress

Caring or cruel? Inside the primate laboratory

The Guardian, given rare access to an animal research facility, talks to scientists about their experiments on monkeys

Anna stares at the computer screen and considers her options. In front of her are two shapes – a flower and a stripy diamond. If she picks the right one she will be rewarded with banana milkshake, but the wrong choice will briefly switch the lights off in her Perspex box. She opts for the diamond and is plunged into darkness.

During the next nine minutes Anna makes the same mistake over and over again. The neuroscientists who designed this experiment are testing how good Anna is at learning new rules. Over the last few weeks she has learned that the diamond was her ticket to a tasty, sugary drink, but this is the first test in which the rules have been reversed. Most of the subjects adapt quickly. But Anna is different.

A marmoset

In March she was subjected to precision brain surgery in which researchers destroyed a small area of her brain. To the untrained eye this has not affected her behaviour at all; she moves, eats and socialises normally. But the experiments are showing that the specific brain region

By James Randerson, Science Correspondent

knocked out is crucial for subtle behavioural abilities.

If Anna was human, this experiment would not be possible. But the studies conducted on her and the other marmosets at one of the most controversial research facilities in the UK are providing vital insights into the brain malfunctions that cause psychiatric conditions such as schizophrenia, obsessive compulsive disorder (OCD), attention deficit hyperactivity disorder (ADHD) and depression.

Critics say using animals in research is simply old-fashioned science

Animal rights campaigners condemn this research as cruel and unnecessary. This week, the renowned primatologist Dr Jane Goodall urged the EU to do more to promote other routes to cures. She advocated a Nobel Prize for alternatives to animal testing. She said: 'We should admit that the infliction of suffering on beings who are capable of feeling is ethically problematic and that the amazing human brain should set to work to find new ways of testing and experimenting that will not involve the use of live, sentient beings.'

The European Commission is reviewing Directive 86/609, which governs animal research across the EU. Goodall and groups who oppose animal experimentation hope to pressure the commission to include a timetable for ending primate testing altogether.

'Primate use is deeply embedded into the system and the prospect of ending it brings significant resistance from some researchers, who have been known to make overblown and unscientific statements about the "critical necessity" of their research,' said a spokesperson for the British Union for the Abolition of Vivisection (BUAV).

The Guardian was granted access to the controversial facility. We were allowed to visit every room in the complex and see every animal on the understanding that we did not reveal its location. The names of workers at the site have been changed to protect their identities.

Despite being a world-class neuroscientist, Jessica, who runs the secret marmoset research facility at a leading UK university, rarely talks openly about her job. 'I very seldom tell anyone what I actually do, because you just don't know who you are talking to,' she said. Police have found her name on a hit list compiled by animal rights extremists and she is afraid that if her involvement becomes more widely known her home and family might be targeted.

To minimise the chance of her identity being revealed, Jessica has never before talked to a journalist. But now she feels a duty to speak. 'I'm fed up with the amount of misinformation that's constantly put out,' she said.

She particularly objects to the photographs on anti-vivisection websites depicting monkeys terrified because protesters have broken in during the night or images that are deliberately cropped to make the cages look tiny. They are often decades out of date, she said. 'The disorders which we are trying to treat are crippling to people. I would love it if we could just tell the world what we do.'

Her anonymous building with mirrored windows looks no different from any other set of academic offices. Inside there is the familiar faint university whiff of the academic coffee room, but here it is mingled with the pungent smell of monkey urine. The marmosets are housed in nine rooms, in cages nearly 3 metres (9ft) high that are full of ladders, beams and ropes. The cages are bespoke, designed specifically with the needs of this species in mind. The monkeys, which are bred on site, live either in family groups of up to 15 or in pairs, as they would in the wild.

'What we try to do is, as closely as possible, give them all the opportunities they would have in the wild,' said Peter, the lab's animal welfare officer. The facility has been visited by marmoset specialists at UK zoos who wanted to learn from the state-of-the-art husbandry that Peter has developed. 'I think a lot of people have the idea that you have mad scientists with primates in cages stuck on their desks. That's just not what it is,' he said.

In the marmoset kitchen, Peter prepares the monkeys' daily menu. Their basic diet consists of egg and Complan sandwiches, along with pellets that give them the correct balance of minerals. But Peter also includes a dried fruit and nut mix, fresh apples, bananas, pears, grapes and peanuts. Farley's rusks,

Heinz banana delight, malt loaf and the marmosets' favourite – mini marshmallows – are also in the larder.

Groups who oppose the use of animals in research claim that scientists force their monkeys to perform by starving them and withholding water. Peter vigorously denied this. Even without the treats they receive during the experiments, he said the animals receive a nutritionally balanced diet. Breeding animals receive exactly the same diet as the experimental monkeys.

'It is restricted. We restrict the times when they have treats. But we are not starving the animals by any stretch of the imagination and we are not dehydrating the animals,' he said. Apart from Peter's desire to treat the animals well and his obligation to do so under the strict husbandry regulations stipulated by the Home Office, he said treating the animals badly would be counter-productive, because animals forced into participating in experiments would give unreliable results.

Every monkey has a numbered collar, but each one also has a name. The colony's family tree goes back to 1978 and each year the researchers choose a theme for the names so that it is easy to tell when a monkey was born. Gin and Tonic, for example are two marmosets from 2005, the drink-themed year. Hermione was

born in 2003 – the Harry Potter year. This year's dual theme is herbs and cars. 'This may sound strange, but I work here because I love animals. It's as simple as that,' Peter said.

For those who oppose primate research though, even the best welfare conditions entail suffering. 'We know that the heightened sentience, intelligence and emotional needs of monkeys make even day-to-day life in a laboratory cage a grave animal welfare issue – quite aside from the horrifying suffering that can be caused by invasive brain studies or protracted poisoning tests,' said the BUAV spokesperson.

And this is the crunch point for many people uneasy about experimenting on the brains of creatures so close in evolutionary terms to ourselves.

To investigate how the monkeys' brains work the researchers must destroy parts of the brain tissue. That involves shaving the marmoset's head, drilling tiny holes into its skull,

Backstory

Research using non-human primates is the most controversial area of animal research, but it accounts for a tiny minority of experiments. No great apes (chimpanzees, orang-utans and gorillas) have been used in experiments in the UK since 1986 and it has been government policy not to use them since 1997. No prosimians (for example, bush babies and lemurs) have been used for several years. Baboons have not been used since 1998. Scientists argue that animal research is highly regulated to ensure it is carried out as humanely as possible. Home Office inspectors make unannounced visits to licensed laboratories to check standards of animal welfare. A five-year licence can take six months of detailed work to put together and submit to the Home Office. The research is expensive. Housing a marmoset for a year costs around £4,000; a larger macaque monkey around £18,000.

inserting a needle and injecting a tiny quantity of toxin. To destroy some brain structures, the scientists must make up to eight brain lesions. All of this happens in an operating theatre on site using equipment and anaesthetic the same as would be used in human brain surgery.

Research using non-human primates is the most controversial area of animal research, but it accounts for a tiny minority of experiments

---

The operations, under anaesthetic, last around three hours. Typically, the marmosets take around four hours to come round, at which point they are reunited with their cage mate. They are monitored as they recover from the anaesthetic and a vet is on call for all the monkeys day and night.

One of the post-doctoral researchers introduces a pair of experimental animals, Anna and Hedwig, that underwent brain surgery in March and April respectively. The fur on Hedwig's head is still growing back, but he is bounding around the cage like all the others. 'You are a mallow monster – yes,' says Sarah in a high-pitched baby voice as she hands a marshmallow through the bars of the cage. She knows 20 animals by sight and said they have unique personalities.

It is Anna's turn for her behavioural test. 'I would honestly say that they like testing. If, for some reason, you don't test one for a day they are not happy with you,' said Sarah. She places a small Perspex box next to an opening in the cage and Anna jumps in immediately to grab the marshmallow on offer. Sarah takes her to the experimental room where Anna spends a few minutes pressing on the computer screen. Despite failing to receive the milkshake, Anna shows no sign of being stressed by the exercise and she is back in her cage with Hedwig within 10 minutes.

The research in the lab is not aimed at testing the effectiveness of specific new drugs against the simian equivalents of human brain diseases or testing how toxic new products are. They are aimed at understanding the basic neural architecture of primates (including us) so that treatments for brain diseases even become a possibility. One focus is on testing the monkeys' behavioural flexibility and finding out which areas of the brain are responsible. It is these parts of the brain that are altered in conditions such as OCD and ADHD.

OCD patients feel compelled to repeat behaviours such as washing their hands. Anna, returning time and again to the wrong symbol in her computer test, is performing the equivalent behaviour, said Jessica. When OCD patients are given the same rule-changing task they act in the same way. The difference with Anna is that it is possible to work out which part of the brain is responsible for the behaviour and so offer options for treating the symptoms in people.

Jessica is adamant that the insights her team is providing into how the human brain works would simply not be possible any other way. 'I really don't believe there is an alternative at the moment,' she said. 'Tissue cultures don't behave. Imaging can't get at cause and effect. Modelling can't work unless you understand what you are trying to model.' No scientist would choose to work on animals unless there was no alternative, she said. It is expensive, bureaucratic and dangerous because of the lengths to which some who oppose the work are prepared to go. 'You need to do something for this huge number of people who suffer from these really debilitating psychiatric disorders. We can't do that unless we understand how the brain controls our behaviour.'

Critics say using animals in research is simply old-fashioned science. 'Urgent action is needed to improve the protection of animals and to replace unethical and outdated animal experiments with non-animal techniques,' said Dr Gill Langley of the Dr Hadwen Trust, a non-animal medical research charity. She favours methods such as tissue culture, computer modelling and brain scans, which she says are more advanced and relevant to human patients.

31 May 2008

© *Guardian Newspapers Limited 2008*

Scientific procedures on animals

Species used in scientific procedures on living animals in Britain, 2007

Species	Numbers	Change since 2006
Procedures on mice (69% of the total)	2,221,981	Up 7%
Procedures on rats	385,654	Down 5%
Procedures on guinea pigs	31,857	Up 5%
Procedures on hamsters	3,371	Down 21%
Procedures on rabbits	19,578	Down 4%
Procedures on horses, donkeys or crossbreeds	8,795	Down 0.3%
Procedures on sheep	32,741	Down 10%
Procedures on pigs	3,192	Down 32%
Procedures on birds	127,637	Up 11%
Procedures on amphibians	18,045	Up 45%
Procedures on reptiles	863	Up 334%
Procedures on fish	327,586	Up 20%
Procedures on cats (individual number of cats: 179)	308	Down 41%
Procedures on primates	3,964	Down 6%
Procedures on dogs (7,276 beagles and 188 crossbreeds)	7,464	Up 9%

Source: Figures have been extracted from the Home Office publication 'Statistics on Scientific Procedures on Living Animals, Great Britain 2007' (published July 2008). Crown copyright.

Respondents were asked: 'In your view, is it acceptable or not acceptable to test new medical treatments on animals before they are tested on human beings?'

Males
- No, it is not acceptable under any circumstances – 10%
- Don't know 8%
- Yes, testing new medical treatments on animals is acceptable 82%

Females
- Don't know 16%
- No, it is not acceptable under any circumstances 25%
- Yes, testing new medical treatments on animals is acceptable 59%

Respondents were asked: 'Some people say that testing new medical treatments on animals is not really necessary and that alternative methods are always available. From what you know, is testing on animals sometimes essential, or are alternative methods always available?'

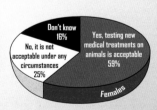

- Testing on animals is sometimes essential – 72%
- Alternative testing methods are always available – 19%
- Don't know – 9%

Sample size: 2102. Fieldwork: 23-25 May 2006. Source: YouGov (www.yougov.com)

Hunting with dogs (fox hunting)

Information from politics.co.uk

What is hunting with dogs?

Hunting with dogs was practised across rural Britain, involving the pursuit and usually killing of animals with one or more dogs, frequently followed by riders on horseback.

A number of different animals were hunted with dogs in the UK, including foxes, deer, hares and mink. Each quarry species was hunted in a different way.

Hunting was regarded variously either as a recreational pastime, a pest-control measure, or a cruel and inhuman blood sport. It was one of the most divisive political issues of recent years. Although all forms of hunting were controversial, fox hunting was the most widespread form of hunting with dogs, and as such, it was the focus of public and political attention.

Background

The hunting of animals with dogs has been a rural activity for centuries. The development of modern fox hunting is believed to have arisen following the Restoration in 1660, and modelled on the royal sport of stag hunting. As stag hunting declined in the 18th century, many stag hunts shifted to fox hunting.

Some farmers have traditionally welcomed hunts on their land for their pest-control functions, but others have been concerned that the environmental damage caused outweighed any pest-control benefits. Proponents of hunting argue that hunts provide an essential service to rural communities, and are an important component of rural culture and the economy.

There has long been opposition to hunting on animal welfare grounds, and during the 1970s and 1980s the activities of 'hunt saboteurs' – who sought to disrupt hunts – increasingly came to prominence with occasional violent clashes with huntsmen.

Hunting became a particularly high-profile political issue in the late 1990s, with the election of Tony Blair's Labour government, which in its 1997 manifesto promised MPs a free vote on a ban on hunting with hounds.

A large number of Labour MPs were very keen to use the party's majority to ban hunting, but the government remained formally neutral. As a result, MPs sought to ban hunting through a number of private members' bills, which failed for lack of parliamentary time.

By 1999 no such free vote on a ban had appeared. The government appointed the Burns inquiry to investigate the practical aspects of the different types of hunting with dogs, the implications of a ban and how any ban might be implemented. The Burns inquiry was not asked to judge whether hunting was cruel.

The resulting report, published in 2000, was seized on by both sides who each claimed it validated their argument. On animal welfare, the Burns report did conclude that hunting 'seriously compromises the welfare of the fox', but it suggested that other methods such as using shotguns during the day or snaring could be considered equally cruel.

It also agreed that hunts did contribute to the cohesion of rural communities, but qualified this by saying that this was not as important as the bonds formed by the village pub or church. In terms of the economic impact of any ban, Burns estimated that there were around 700 jobs directly associated with hunting, and a total of 6,000 to 8,000 jobs dependent on it.

However, he qualified this by saying that 'in terms of national resource use, the economic effects of a ban on hunting would be unlikely to be substantial', with the effects most likely to have dissipated within a decade, but that in the short term 'the individual and local effects would be more serious'.

- HOW'S THE BAN ON HUNTING BILL GOING??

... DON'T HOLD YOUR BREATH...

In response, the government pursued a number of bills that would give parliament a free vote on a number of options: an outright ban, hunting with regulations, and maintaining the status quo. In each case, the bill failed due to irreconcilable differences and the impossibility of getting a bill that satisfied the Commons through the House of Lords.

The Labour government made a manifesto commitment in 2001 to resolve the contentious issue of hunting with dogs in England and Wales. The rural affairs minister, Alun Michael, introduced a new hunting bill in December 2002 which would have banned stag hunting and hare coursing and introduced a system of licensing for fox hunting. Hunts would be eligible to register if they could show that hunting was undertaken for purposes specific to pest control (the utility test), and that it would cause less suffering than any alternative method of pest control (the cruelty test).

This bill, however, met opposition in the Commons and the Lords. The Commons amended the bill to push for an outright ban, but this was then amended to a licensing system by the Lords. It was then re-amended to a ban by the Commons, before being finally rejected by the Lords. Eventually, the bill ran out of time.

Hunting with dogs was banned in Scotland by a 2002 Act of the Scottish parliament, which was two years in the completion.

In 2004 the government re-introduced the issue and gave MPs a free vote to pass an outright ban on hunting with dogs. The leader of the House, Peter Hain, made the decision to rush the bill through the Commons in a single day – drawing protests from pro-hunting groups and politicians. The bill was, however, comprehensively backed by the House and was sent to the Lords with the government warning that an outright rejection would be met with the Parliament Act.

The Parliament Act of 1949 gives the House of Commons the ability to pass legislation even if the House of Lords has rejected it twice, but only after a year has passed since the Commons first introduced the bill.

The act is controversial because it was not initially passed by both the Lords and the Commons.

In November 2004 the Commons decided to invoke the Parliament Act to ban fox hunting outright in England and Wales after weeks of legislative ping-pong between the two houses. The Lords repeatedly voted to allow hunting to continue under licence, but this was rejected by the Commons.

But on the last day of debate, the government attempted to amend the bill to delay implementation of the ban to July 2007. MPs rejected this, agreeing to July 2006 instead. This presented the House of Lords with a dilemma.

Hunting with dogs has been one of the most controversial issues of recent times

If they voted for the bill the ban would have been delayed until July 2006. This would be good for pro-hunting campaigners but it would have let the government off the hook by relieving them of the need to use the Parliament Act and to introduce a potentially unpopular ban just months before a general election in May 2005.

Another choice was to vote for an amended bill that would allow fox hunting to continue under licence. Peers chose this option, and, as a result, the government enacted the Parliament Act. The bill was forced through on 18 November 2004, stipulating a full ban on fox hunting, deer hunting and hare coursing to come into effect in February 2005.

Controversies

Hunting with dogs has been one of the most controversial issues of recent times. There were essentially three positions represented in the debate: those who wanted hunting to continue in its present form; those who wanted it banned; and those who wanted hunting to continue, but with regulation to mitigate its negative effects.

The principal exponent of keeping hunting in its present form is the Countryside Alliance (CA). In the opposing camp is Campaigning to Protect Hunted Animals (CPHA), made up of the Royal Society for the Protection of Cruelty to Animals (RSPCA), the League Against Cruel Sports and the International Fund for Animal Welfare (IFAW).

The regulated approach was promoted by the Middle Way Group, a small but vocal cross-party group of MPs. Neither Labour nor the Conservative party has an official position on hunting – all the votes of recent years have been free votes, as hunting is regarded as an issue of conscience. However, most Conservatives have historically voted in support of hunting, while a smaller majority of Labour and Liberal Democrat MPs have voted against it.

Central to the controversy is a tension between the anti-hunt campaigners' protestations of cruelty with the pro-hunters' assertions that hunting is an integral part of rural life. Animal welfare campaigners argue that animals are literally torn apart by dogs, and fervently reject the hunters' claims that animals are killed quickly. This principle argument has, however, spun off countless sub-debates on what level of pest foxes are; what damage is caused by hunts to the countryside; and what freedoms and liberties the individual has. In recent months, the Countryside Alliance has repeatedly accused the anti-hunt MPs of a form of class warfare.

Fox hunting has also emerged as a symbol of tensions between urban and rural Britain. This culminated in the September 2002 'Liberty and Livelihood' March through London, organised by the Countryside Alliance, when an estimated 400,000 people demonstrated in support of rural concerns, chief among which was keeping fox hunting.

In late 2004, as the prospect of the ban moved closer, some pro-hunting demonstrations increasingly took on a violent element. Sixteen individuals were arrested on 15 September when a demonstration turned violent outside parliament, while inside the House of Commons hunt protesters

The use of animals by society

The pie chart below shows the number of animals used in the UK in one year. The major areas are for food, as companion animals (pets), in medical research and those destroyed as pests (mostly rats and mice), and those cats and dogs abandoned and destroyed by animal welfare organisations.

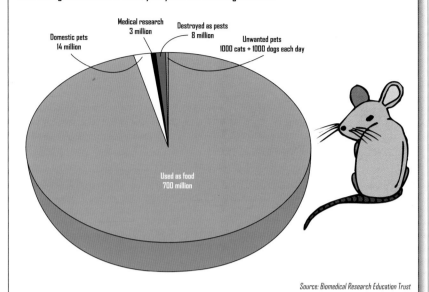

Domestic pets
14 million

Medical research
3 million

Destroyed as pests
8 million

Unwanted pets
1000 cats + 1000 dogs each day

Used as food
700 million

Source: Biomedical Research Education Trust

broke into the chamber but were quickly detained. Later that month carcasses of dead animals were dumped in Brighton outside the Labour party conference. Although the mainstream Countryside Alliance distanced itself from these activities, it published the *Hunting Handbook* outlining loopholes in the Hunting Act which allow hunts to continue while operating completely inside the law. The League Against Cruel Sports responded by establishing the Hunt Crime Watch programme designed to help provide police with information so that they may easily prosecute those violating the Hunting Act.

In the political arena, some backbenchers and commentators began to question the amount of parliamentary time dedicated to the issue, at the expense of other matters. Anti-hunt campaigners believed that banning hunting was a moral issue upon which there could be no compromise and welcomed the decision of the Commons to vote for an outright ban and ignore 'compromise' proposals.

After the bill came into effect in February 2005, pro-hunt campaigners sought to contest the Hunting Act using two legal challenges: the validity of the 1949 Parliament Act; and on the basis that the ban infringed their human rights. Leading this fight was the Countryside Alliance. In October that year, it was decided unanimously by nine law lords that the 1949 Act had been used by the House of Commons in accordance with the law.

In August 2006, Exmoor Foxhounds' huntsman Tony Wright became the first person to be convicted of illegally hunting a fox under the terms of the act. He was fined £500 and ordered to pay £250 costs after a week-long trial at Barnstaple magistrates' court.

But questions remain about whether the ban is being, or can be, implemented effectively. Countryside Alliance chief executive Simon Hart stated in May 2008: 'Most hunts have been able to carry out a range of hunting activities with only a very few facing vindictive prosecutions. The courts, meanwhile, are struggling to make sense of the legislation and it will be some time yet before they properly define the law, if they ever do.'

Statistics
A survey of over 2,000 people carried out in 2008 on behalf of the International Fund for Animal Welfare, the RSPCA and the League Against Cruel Sports found that:

When people were asked about their views on whether fox hunting should be made legal again, almost three-quarters, 73%, said it should remain illegal.

A second survey asked whether people felt that those who currently take part in hunting with dogs – despite it being illegal – should be allowed to do so. Around seven in ten, 71%, said hunters should not be allowed to break the law.

Source: Ipsos MORI 29/02/08

Quotes
'Hunters cannot ride roughshod over the Hunting Act. It's only a matter of time before the minority who illegally chase and kill animals for pleasure will be brought to justice.'
Douglas Batchelor, chief executive of the League Against Cruel Sport, February 2008
'There are more reasons to be positive about the future of hunting now than at any time for a decade. Our opponents did their worst and the Hunting Act finally became law, yet the infrastructure of hunting is largely undented.'
Countryside Alliance chief executive Simon Hart, May 2008
'Hunting or baiting wild animals is cruel and unacceptable and has no place in modern society.'
RSPCA chief inspector, Ian Briggs, May 2008
'After years of discussion, parliament decided that fox hunting should be banned. Is not the priority now to ensure that the legislation is implemented effectively, and not to promise that it will be repealed at some date in the future?'
Labour MP Paddy Tipping questioning Gordon Brown at PMQs, April 2008
'I understand that the leader of the opposition has said: "We would let the House of Commons have a free vote... and...if there was a vote to get rid of the ban...there would be a government bill in government time."

'I believe that there is a settled view among the public on the matter and that it would be better if all parties in the House recognised the previous vote of the House of Commons on the issue.'
Gordon Brown's response to Paddy Tipping's question.

⇨ The above information is reprinted with kind permission from politics.co.uk. Visit www.politics.co.uk for more information.
© Adfero

Hunting Act 2004: the case for repeal

Information from the Countryside Alliance

Introduction

The Hunting Act came into force on 18 February 2005 after an eight-year battle that absorbed over 700 hours of Parliamentary time. The prejudice, misuse of science and abuse of parliamentary process that eventually saw the Act onto the statute book were the focus of criticism and regret from politicians of all parties, the media and the public.

> **The Hunting Act came into force on 18 February 2005 after an eight-year battle that absorbed over 700 hours of Parliamentary time**

The Hunting Act is unique in that its effects are entirely negative. It diminishes respect for Parliament; it puts law-abiding people at risk of prosecution; it diverts police attention from real crime; it brings no benefit to the environment; it is a blatant example of political prejudice and it does nothing for the welfare or conservation of the species it claims to 'protect'.

The question now is not whether hunting should, or should not, have been banned, but whether the Hunting Act is a piece of legislation that should remain on the statute book. In other words, should the Act be repealed?

This document makes the 'Case for Repeal'. It is a powerful, convincing argument. The Hunting Act is a law that fails at every level – it is badly drafted, illiberal, cruel and divisive. Scrapping the Act need not be complicated or time consuming. In fact it could be remarkably simple. Public and political support for the Act has fallen dramatically and it is possible that a future Parliament is likely to have a majority of MPs who support its repeal. When that time comes, this 'Case for Repeal' is the justification that a Government, of whatever colour, will need to consign the Hunting Act to the dustbin of British history.

A confusing law

From the outset, the practical application of the Hunting Act has been surrounded by confusion. According to the Government, hunting can only be an 'intentional' activity. So it is the intention of a person engaged with a dog or dogs, not the action of those dogs, which is criminal. The fact that a dog is pursuing a fox, or another mammal, does not necessarily mean that an offence is being committed.

The series of 'exemptions' designed to allow some types of hunting to continue were the result of political wrangling and are both illogical and unclear. For instance it is legal to hunt a rabbit, but not a hare; a rat, but not a mouse. It is legal to use two dogs to flush to a waiting gun, but not three.

It is legal to use any number of dogs in order to flush a mammal (unspecified) for a bird of prey (also unspecified). It is legal to use a terrier underground to control foxes because they are killing game birds, but illegal to use the same dog to kill the same fox if it is killing lambs. Defining these exemptions has been left to huntsmen, the police and the courts.

The Hunting Act carries a maximum fine of £5,000 which gives it the same status as a minor road traffic violation. The police have said that they will investigate allegations of illegal hunting, but that they can only police hunting in the context of existing policing priorities. The situation is made more difficult by the continued harassment of a few hunts by animal rights activists. Unfounded allegations of Hunting Act offences are wasting police time and resources that could be spent tackling real crimes that affect the lives of ordinary people.

They said it . . .

'I might have been found guilty but I certainly don't feel like a criminal. We had two hounds; a marksman and we shot a fox. I don't know what else we were supposed to do to comply with the law.'

Tony Wright, huntsman of the Exmoor Foxhounds, on being the first huntsman to be convicted under the Hunting Act, 4th August 2006.

'Parliament's vote for an outright ban on hunting with dogs fills many of my fellow officers with dread. Not because the police are pro-hunting – the service is determinedly neutral – but because of the practical implications of enforcing such a ban.'

Alastair McWhirter, Chief Constable of Suffolk and ACPO spokesman on hunting, The Times, 3rd July 2003.

'The intentions or actions of the hunter determine what is going on. Hunting has an ordinary English meaning: "to hunt" is the intention to pursue a wild mammal. Without that intent, a person is not hunting and is not covered by the offence.'

Defra Minister Alun Michael, Hunting Bill Committee, 4th February 2003.

'We observe at the outset that the experience of this case has led us to the conclusion that the (Hunting Act) is far from simple to interpret or to apply: it seems to us that any given set of facts may be susceptible to differing interpretations. The result is an unhappy state of affairs which leaves all those involved in a position of uncertainty.'

Judge Graham Cottle and two lay magistrates overturning the conviction of Tony Wright. Exeter Crown Court, 30th November 2007.

'Less than three in ten (29%) of UK adults think the Hunting Act is working.'

Opinion Research Business poll, September 2006.

'Unfortunately the wording of the Act is ambiguous.'

Professor Patrick Bateson appearing as a witness for the League Against Cruel Sports against the Quantocks Staghounds, 22nd May 2007.

An illiberal law

Despite claims to the contrary, the Hunting Act never had the support of Parliament. In fact, more parliamentarians voted against it than for it. The Hunting Act was eventually driven through the House of Commons in a single day following a blatant breach of Parliamentary protocol. It was then forced past the House of Lords using the ultimate constitutional sledgehammer, the Parliament Acts, which were used for only the fourth time since 1949.

The measure of a true democracy is tolerance: tolerance of minorities, and tolerance of activities that the majority might not support. Legislation, especially legislation that prohibits an activity of profound cultural importance, should be considered only if it can be proved to remove a demonstrable harm. Despite years of consultation and debate, and a Government inquiry, there was never any evidence that hunting created that harm. There is, however, considerable evidence that the motivation of many who supported the Act was straightforward prejudice and the settling of old political scores.

As long as the Hunting Act remains on the statute book, it will be a challenge to Britain's claim to be a tolerant and moderate society.

They said it . . .

'This is what happens when democracy goes wrong.'

BBC Political Editor Andrew Marr during a pro-hunt demonstration in Parliament Square, 15th September 2004.

'Now that hunting has been banned, we ought at last to own up to it: the struggle over the Bill was not just about animal welfare and personal freedom, it was class war.'

Peter Bradley MP, PPS to Defra Minister

Alun Michael, Sunday Telegraph, 21st November 2004.

'Tony, if you invoke the Parliament Act it will be the most illiberal act of the last century.'

Former Labour Home Secretary and mentor to Tony Blair, Roy Jenkins, to Blair shortly before Lord Jenkins' death in January 2003.

'Such a bad law has no right to survive and it would be better to get rid of it.'

Sunday Times editorial, 12th February 2006.

'Naturally, people ask whether we were implying that hunting is cruel... the short answer to that question is no. There was not sufficient verifiable evidence or data safely to reach views about cruelty.'

Lord Burns, Chairman of the Inquiry into Hunting with Dogs. House of Lords, 12th March 2001.

'I struggle to see how the Hunting Act 2004 passes the Minister, Alun Michael's, test that the legislation should be soundly based on evidence and principle and that it should stand the test of time.'

Lord Burns, Chairman of the Inquiry into Hunting with Dogs, House of Lords, 12th October 2004.

A cruel law

The Hunting Act does not protect wild mammals from unnecessary suffering, nor does it promote their conservation. It simply tries to prohibit certain methods of wildlife management despite the fact that there is no scientific evidence that they are any less humane than the alternatives. The impact of the Hunting Act has actually been that more foxes, deer and hares are being killed.

The Act limits the options available to farmers and land managers for controlling and managing wild mammals, which makes it difficult to find animals that are suffering and in distress and almost impossible to protect lambs and other livestock in some areas.

Hunting has also played a crucial role in the creation and management of the British countryside for centuries. The Act threatens the conservation work that hunts, and land managers who support hunting, have carried out for generations. Given the difficulties that the Hunting Act creates for wildlife management, animal welfare and biodiversity it is no surprise that the Government is not measuring the impact of its legislation.

They said it . . .

'Landowners who hunt with hounds are more likely to conserve woodland habitat and plant more woodland and hedgerows, suggesting that the perceived recreation and social benefits of this controversial activity can produce conservation benefits.'
T. E. E. Oldfield, R. J. Smith, S. R. Harrop & N. Leader-Williams. Durrell Institute of Conservation and Ecology, University of Kent. Nature Magazine 29th May 2003.

'36% – The proportion of hunts counting fewer foxes since the Hunting Act came into force.'
Masters of Foxhounds Association survey October 2006.

'19% – The reduction in red deer numbers on Exmoor from 2005 to 2006.'
Exmoor Deer Management Group annual counts.

'The Government have no plans to evaluate the effects of the Hunting Act.'
Defra Minister Ben Bradshaw, House of Commons, 24th May 2005.

'Pairs of dogs are utterly useless in flushing to guns.'
Douglas Batchelor, Chief Executive of the League Against Cruel Sports, admits in a leaked memo that the Hunting Act is not working for gun packs, August 2005.

'Describing, as we did, the final moments of a hunt as "seriously compromising the welfare of the hunted animal" should not be taken as a suggestion that hunting was measurably worse than other legal methods, or that abolition would improve the plight of wild animals in the countryside.'
Professor Sir John Marsh and Professor Michael Winter, members of the Committee of Inquiry into Hunting with Dogs, a letter to Environment Minister Margaret Beckett, May 2005.

A divisive law

When historians come to judge Tony Blair's legacy for the countryside one issue will dominate their thoughts: the long, wasteful and irrelevant battle over hunting legislation. At a time of profound social and economic change in rural communities it was this issue that dominated the Government's agenda and cemented the view that it did not understand, or care, about the real issues of the countryside. Worse, it became quite clear that the Prime Minister knew that there were other more pressing issues, but was too weak to pursue them.

An administration determined to tackle real rural issues like plummeting farm incomes, disappearing rural services and the increasingly unaffordable cost of basic commodities like housing and fuel would not have wasted so much time and effort on the Hunting Act. Repealing the Act and removing the running sore at the heart of rural policy need not be complicated or time consuming, and even anti-hunting politicians are increasingly seeing its demise as inevitable.

A Government determined to focus on working for the countryside could send no clearer signal than scrapping the Hunting Act.

They said it . . .

'Blair may bleat on about his legacy but as far as I can see he'll be best remembered as the man who spent too much time on an unworkable anti-hunting Bill.'
John Gaunt, The Sun, 27th December 2005.

'Be clear. Only one argument matters on hunting: that it doesn't matter... if politics is the language of priorities, then our politicians have never got it so badly wrong.'
New Statesman editorial, 7th July 2003.

'As a Liberal, I cannot find it in me to declare that fox hunting should be a criminal offence.'
Sir Menzies Campbell MP, former Leader of the Liberal Democrats, 23rd September 2002.

'The future of our society should be founded on shared values of liberty and democracy and fairness.'
Prime Minister Gordon Brown MP, 12th January 2007. 0 – number of times Gordon Brown voted for the Hunting Act.

'We'd give MPs a free vote on overturning the hunting ban and if the vote went through there'd be a Government Bill to get rid of it. I mean, my own view is that the ban isn't working. It's a farce really.'
David Cameron MP, Leader of the Opposition, 1st May 2007.

'Hunts are carrying on because they are waiting for a change, which they think will take place at the next general election. They hope that the legislation will then be repealed, which is even greater reason to make their lives uncomfortable between now and then.'
Ann Widdecombe MP, House of Commons, 22nd March 2007.
20 November 2008

⇨ The above information is reprinted with kind permission from the Countryside Alliance. Visit www.countryside-alliance.org.uk for more information on this and related issues.

© *Countryside Alliance*

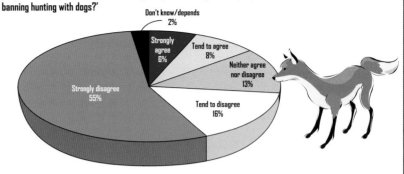

Public opinion on hunting with dogs

Respondents were asked: 'Now a question about hunting with dogs (that is, fox hunting, deer hunting, stag hunting and hare hunting and coursing). Hunting with dogs is illegal in Great Britain – but despite this sometimes people still take part. To what extent do you agree or disagree that people should be allowed to break the law banning hunting with dogs?'

Don't know/depends 2%
Strongly agree 6%
Tend to agree 8%
Neither agree nor disagree 13%
Strongly disagree 55%
Tend to disagree 16%

Base: Results based on 2,007 face-to-face interviews with adults aged 15+ in Great Britain across 181 sampling points. Data is weighted to known profile of Great Britain. Fieldwork: 8-14 February 2008.
Source: Ipsos MORI, 29 February 2008.

Hunting

Information from Animal Aid

Victory! In February 2005, hunting with packs of dogs became illegal. This means that hunts cannot encourage a pack of hounds to chase a fox and then rip the fox to pieces. Mink hunting has also been banned, as has hare coursing and stag hunting.

This is a huge and long overdue step towards eliminating animal cruelty. It remains to be seen whether hunts will abide by the law, or break the law and face prosecution.

What was hunting all about?

The hunting of wild animals (such as red deer, wild boar, hares and wolves) with dogs was a traditional 'sport' of kings and rich landowners. When wild boars and wolves became extinct, and the deer herds declined, hunters wanted a new 'quarry' (the name given to the animal who is chased) – the fox. Around 8-10,000 cubs and 10-12,000 adults met this fate each year. Fox hunting existed for 250 years. The official fox hunting season began on 1 November and ended in April, although some hunts would hunt until May.

From August until September hunters would chase fox cubs in order to get the new hounds used to the smell of foxes. The dogs (or hounds, as they are known) did not hunt foxes by instinct, but had to be trained and encouraged to do so. The hounds who were not good enough at hunting would be killed. The same happened to hounds considered too old to hunt – at just five or six years of age!

The current situation

Even though hunting with dogs has been banned, hunts are allowed to send two hounds into a wood to 'flush out' a diseased fox into the open. And terriermen can 'dig out' a fox who has 'gone to ground', and shoot him or her dead.

So why did people go hunting?

'Foxes are pests who need to be controlled'

Foxes are often accused of killing chickens, but as the vast majority of chickens are imprisoned indoors in intensive 'battery' and 'broiler' units, few are in any danger from foxes. Hens who are free-range can easily be fenced in and/or securely locked up at night to keep them safe. Foxes are also accused of killing lambs, although the government agrees that less than 1% of all lamb mortalities are caused by foxes. Foxes are scavengers by nature and so tend to take lambs who are already dead. According to government figures, around 15% of newborn lambs die, principally from starvation, disease or exposure.

'Hunting is the most humane way to control foxes'

Hunting was not the most humane way to 'control' foxes. Foxes do not, in any case, need to be 'controlled' by people killing them. They are a valuable part of the British landscape, and their numbers are controlled naturally by how much food and suitable habitat is available. In 2001, hunting was suspended because of the outbreak of foot and mouth disease, and the government was worried that it would be spread far afield by horses being ridden across wide areas. During that period, when hunts were not allowed to chase and kill foxes, there was no increase in fox numbers. All the different ways that are used to kill foxes, such as snares, shooting, gassing, trapping and poisoning, are cruel and unnecessary. However, hunting was the only method that was designed to be cruel. The whole point of hunting was that the chase lasted as long as possible. That was why the hounds were selectively bred to have stamina and to run for a long time, instead of the hunt using dogs who could sprint for a short time (e.g. greyhounds). Not only was the chase exhausting and terrifying, but the final kill was violent and painful. If the fox tried to take refuge underground, for example in an earth or in a drain, then small, fierce terrier dogs would be sent down to fight with, and drive out, the fox to his or her death.

'Hunters preserve the countryside – they are conservationists'

Conservation was not what hunts were all about. The damage done to the countryside as the hunt churned up the ground, and as the followers blasted around the countryside in polluting four-wheel drives, can hardly be classed as considerate to the environment. Farmers are now paid by the government to conserve habitats such as natural woodland, so this is no longer a justification for hunting.

'Banning hunting will cause a loss of jobs, and lead to dogs being killed'

'Drag hunting' would employ the same number of people as traditional hunting. The hunt and the hounds follow a pre-laid false scent – usually composed of animal urine, droppings or an animal corpse. The scented cloth or animal remains will, typically, be dragged behind a mounted rider about half an hour before the hunt wants to set off. A switch to drag hunting means there is no excuse for killing the hounds. Unemployed hounds can always continue to be cared for by those who previously used them for hunting – or they can be rehomed.

What you can do

⇨ Help Animal Aid to achieve a ban on other bloodsports – such as shooting and fishing. Order our Stop Shooting Action Pack and our Angling Factsheet and stickers.

⇨ Join Animal Aid's youth group, Youth4Animals, and help campaign against hunting.

⇨ The above information is reprinted with kind permission from Animal Aid. Visit www.animalaid.org.uk for more information.

© Animal Aid

Hunting after the ban

Has the hunting ban renewed interest in a threatened way of life? Three years after hunting was banned Louise Gray went out with the Puckeridge Hunt on the first day of the open season to see the sport thriving despite the new laws

The hounds are baying, the horses are stamping their hooves and the port is being passed around at Puckeridge Hunt.

It is a pastoral scene in rural Hertfordshire being played out in more than 200 villages across Britain as the hunting season opens.

> **Since hunting with hounds was outlawed three years ago the blood sport has had to think of increasingly creative ways to keep going without killing anything**

But something is different. The hounds are not baying for blood – that would be illegal – but for fox urine imported from America. Since hunting with hounds was outlawed three years ago the blood sport has had to think of increasingly creative ways to keep going without killing anything.

The most popular choice is 'trail hunting' where scent from a boiled fox if you happen to have one handy, or fox urine – which for some bizarre reason is harvested in the States where they keep caged foxes – is laid down for the hounds to follow like a real hunt.

Look closely and the followers of the hunt are also different. Some of the women have their hair down – shock, horror – a look that would never have been allowed in the old days of hair nets and stiff upper lips.

It seems the dress code has relaxed as this most proper of pastimes has been forced to look beyond the country set for support. Many hunts have even ditched the traditional 'pink' jackets, that tend to draw unwanted attention, for more practical tweeds and even waterproofs.

The police car around the corner, the animal rights 'monitors' in luminescent jackets and a general atmosphere of defiance all serve to remind us that in fact hunting is a very different sport since it technically became illegal.

Yet, despite losing status, glamour – and indeed the official reason for its existence – killing foxes – the hunt is more popular than ever.

Perhaps the biggest reason for this is hunting has never been just about killing foxes.

'The politicians thought the huntsmen would just disappear and take up golf but that was never going to happen,' says Tim Bonner of the Countryside Alliance.

'Hunting is a way of life.'

For this reason, since the ban came in hunting has enjoyed support not only from the minority who enjoy the sport but a large part of the countryside community.

'British people do not like to see minorities squeezed by the government,' says Alan Herbert, chairman of the Puckeridge hunt supporters' club.

Like most hunts the Puckeridge has a loyal following of ladies in Barbours with expensive binoculars but also nurses, lorry drivers and village locals passing around a hip flask and enjoying a gossip.

Lauren Jones, who runs a local stables, says there has also been an increase in followers on horseback.

'I have seen a huge increase in the popularity of hunting,' she says. 'It is such an old-fashioned sport that has been going for generations and generations. People want to know what it is all about and experience it. They want to support it not see it lost for ever.'

In many ways hunting has the ban to thank for this renewed interest as people got passionate about a threatened way of life.

The Countryside Alliance reckon support is up 10 per cent this year. Saddlers report increased sales of hunting gear and stables cannot provide enough horses for new recruits.

It is estimated up to 50,000 people will be out hunting every weekend until the end of the season in March, up to 100,000 if the hunt supporters are added.

Mr Bonner admits that in many ways the publicity from the ban has forced a closed society into the modern world.

'Hunting has had a bad image for the last six or seven years – some of it self-inflicted. Since the ban the sport has had to look at itself and open up a bit and become more accessible.'

Louise Hoadley, 29, a single mother who rides out with the East Essex Hunt, says hunting is no longer just for toffs.

'It has lost that stigma,' she says. 'We have all sorts with our hunt. Teachers, farmers, dentists, school children, policemen, even dustbin men.'

It is women like Miss Hoadley who the hunt have to thank for their increasing popularity. Riding is a massive and growing industry in the UK among women aged from their mid 20s to late 50s. Most of the 'field' out with the Puckeridge and across the country are women, while children are also being encouraged to take part.

The fact is that the ban has almost made the sport more legitimate. It means enthusiastic riders can enjoy galloping across the countryside without worrying about turning away during the kill – or indeed explaining themselves later down the pub.

This is something the Countryside Alliance will never admit. The organisation cling to the belief that 'real' hunting will one day return.

They claim that the law is bad for the countryside, not only in putting kennels and other industries that rely on hunting out of business, but for pest control because foxes are being shot in greater numbers by landowners.

Ironically the anti-hunt saboteurs or 'sabs' as they are fondly known also claim the law is a joke, insisting that the hunts continue to 'accidentally' kill foxes during trail hunts. Indeed the law is almost impossible to police and so far there have been only two successful convictions out of 30 prosecutions for breaches of the Hunting Act.

So even though hunting is enjoying continued popularity it is still under threat. Privately the hunting lobby fear that although numbers are going up, the continued risk of breaking the law if a fox is killed – albeit 'accidentally' – means that fewer and fewer people will come forward to finance or lead the hounds – even if there are willing followers.

The only hope is to have the law repealed by a change of government. The Conservative Party have promised to overturn the law if they get in and the hunting lobby will be campaigning hard on their behalf.

'People love their hunting and their hounds,' says Mr Bonner. 'There is absolute determination we will not let this way of life die and there is light at the end of the tunnel now. There is a lot of optimism we can get the law repealed.

'There is hope people will not have the threat of prosecution hanging over them for no reason other than the politicians chose to pick on us.'
10 November 2008
© Telegraph Group Limited, London 2008

Is the ban working?

Information from the International Fund for Animal Welfare

'The assault was the worst that I've suffered during my twenty years of monitoring, but it did not deter me from doing my job. I hope that that verdict and sentence will send a message to hunt supporters that acts of intimidation and violence will not be tolerated. Hunts claim to be obeying the Hunting Act – if this is true then their supporters should have no objection to their activities being observed by hunt monitors.'
Kevin Hill, IFAW hunt monitor

IFAW has been working with police forces throughout the UK since the ban and has expanded its team of hunt monitors. There have been successful prosecutions for illegal hunting and others are pending, including several based on evidence obtained by our WCIs.

IFAW's hunt monitors follow hunts as closely as possible on foot and in vehicles using public land, roads, footpaths and bridleways. They peacefully observe and document their activities, working without any form of intervention. Unfortunately they are often targeted by hunt members and followers: they have received verbal abuse, threats of violence, actual violence and damage to their vehicles. The reluctance of some hunters to be filmed inevitably raises suspicions as to the legality of their activities.

The harassment and intimidation endured by hunt monitors in England and Wales has increased dramatically following successful prosecutions for illegal hunting, which shows that the law indeed has teeth.

IFAW has a number of specific concerns that are currently being pursued with the enforcement authorities. Too many hunts are claiming 'accidental' kills of foxes while trail hunting, a form of hunting in which the scent of a dead fox or fox urine is used to lay a route for the dogs. Out-of-control dogs have also chased and attacked pets and livestock and even invaded homes and gardens. This would not happen if hunts were to adopt drag hunting, in which an artificial (i.e. non-fox) scent is followed.

IFAW has advised police that they should be suspicious if hunts try to defend themselves from allegations of illegal hunting by saying that their dogs were out of control. For centuries hunters have prided themselves on their ability to control their packs. If, for some sudden and inexplicable reason, they are now unable to reliably exert control they should not be out with their dogs.

Regrettably it seems that some hunters have replaced the thrill of the chase with the thrill of trying to get round the law. As convictions for illegal hunting mount it will be interesting to see how long the thrill will last.

⇨ The above information is reprinted with kind permission from the International Fund for Animal Welfare. IFAW seeks to motivate the public to prevent cruelty to animals and to promote animal welfare and conservation policies that advance the wellbeing of both animals and people. Visit www.ifaw.org for more information.
© International Fund for Animal Welfare

Public opinion on hunting with dogs

Information from Ipsos MORI

Two recent surveys of over 2,000 people in Britain were carried out in February by Ipsos MORI for the International Fund for Animal Welfare (IFAW), the RSPCA and the League Against Cruel Sports.

The first survey (Note 1) found that when people were asked about their views on whether certain – currently illegal – hunting activities should be made legal again, that on fox hunting, nearly three-quarters, 73%, said fox hunting should remain illegal, while nearly a quarter, 22%, felt it should be made legal. Comparable figures for deer hunting were 81% vs 12% and for hare hunting and coursing 82% vs 12%.

The reintroduction of dog fighting (96% opposed) and badger baiting (93%) were opposed by the greatest percentage of the public.

The second survey (Note 2) asked whether people felt that those who currently take part in hunting with dogs – despite it being illegal – should be allowed to do so.

Around seven in ten (71%) said they believed that hunters should not be allowed to break the law, while 15% felt they should.

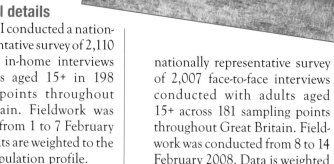

Technical details

1 Ipsos MORI conducted a nationally representative survey of 2,110 face-to-face in-home interviews with adults aged 15+ in 198 sampling points throughout Great Britain. Fieldwork was conducted from 1 to 7 February 2008. Results are weighted to the 15+ GB population profile.

2 Ipsos MORI conducted a nationally representative survey of 2,007 face-to-face interviews conducted with adults aged 15+ across 181 sampling points throughout Great Britain. Fieldwork was conducted from 8 to 14 February 2008. Data is weighted to the known profile of Great Britain.

On fox hunting, nearly three-quarters, 73%, said fox hunting should remain illegal, while nearly a quarter, 22%, felt it should be made legal

Please note: where results do not sum to 100%, this will be due to the omission of those who said they didn't know, or may be due to multiple responses or computer rounding. *29 February 2008*

⇨ The above information is reprinted with kind permission from Ipsos MORI. Visit www.ipsos-mori.com for more information.

© *Ipsos MORI*

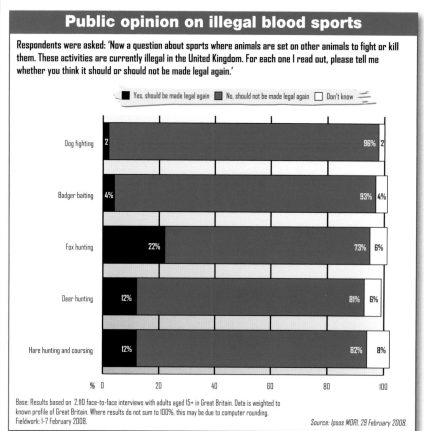

Public opinion on illegal blood sports

Respondents were asked: 'Now a question about sports where animals are set on other animals to fight or kill them. These activities are currently illegal in the United Kingdom. For each one I read out, please tell me whether you think it should or should not be made legal again.'

Legend: ■ Yes, should be made legal again ■ No, should not be made legal again □ Don't know

Category	Yes	No	Don't know
Dog fighting	2	96%	2
Badger baiting	4%	93%	4%
Fox hunting	22%	73%	6%
Deer hunting	12%	81%	6%
Hare hunting and coursing	12%	82%	8%

% 0   20   40   60   80   100

Base: Results based on 2,110 face-to-face interviews with adults aged 15+ in Great Britain. Data is weighted to known profile of Great Britain. Where results do not sum to 100%, this may be due to computer rounding.
Fieldwork: 1-7 February 2008.

Source: Ipsos MORI, 29 February 2008.

Cut the bullfighting

Green MEP Caroline Lucas explains why she thinks that, despite its ancient history, the cruelty of bullfighting can never be justified and calls on the EU to cut its subsidy

In the European Parliament this week, I chaired an open seminar on the future of bullfighting in the EU. Although its organisers originate from varying backgrounds – European animal welfare, veterinary science and economics – they all agree on one thing: bullfighting has to go.

Despite a considerable number of states having banned the practice of bullfighting by law – Argentina, Canada, Cuba, Denmark, Germany, Italy, the Netherlands, New Zealand and the United Kingdom among them – it still takes place in nine countries around the world. This is nine countries too many. Yet it is encouraging to find that even where bullfighting is legal, certain regions have begun to phase it out, such as the Canary Islands in Spain, and most of France.

Public appetite for this cruel blood sport has long been on the wane, but that doesn't stop the Spanish government from heavily subsidising the declining industry. It has been estimated that over 550 million euros of taxpayer money is allocated to the pro-bullfighting industry per year, even though Spanish broadcaster RTVE stopped live coverage of bullfights in August 2007 and recent Gallup polls showed that the majority of Spaniards either disliked bullfighting or had no interest in it. Worse still, the EU subsidises it. According to recent reports, breeders of fighting bulls receive 220 euros per bull per year from the EU, on top of national subsidies. Yet the EU is supposed to be a community of values – one of which is a high level of animal protection.

A cruel and unequal game

The pro-bullfighting lobby puts forward a number of claims for the preservation of the 'sport', which need to be addressed. First, though, it is worth considering the reality of a typical Spanish-style bullfight. The 'show' begins when the bull enters the arena and is provoked into charging several times, before being approached by picadores, men on blindfolded horses, who drive lances into its back and neck muscles. The subsequent loss of blood impairs the bull's ability to lift its head, and when the banderilleros arrive on foot, the bull can expect further pain from the banderillas, spiked sticks in bright colours, being stabbed into its back.

Now weak and disorientated, the bull is encouraged by the banderilleros to run in dizzying circles before finally, the matador appears and, after a few forced charges, tries to kill the bull with his sword. If he misses, he stabs the submissive animal on the back of the neck until it is paralysed. The idea is to cut the animal's spinal cord, but if the matador botches the job, the bull may be fully conscious while its ears or tail are removed as trophies. On many occasions, the bull remains alive until it is dragged out of the arena to be slaughtered

Thousands of bulls are maimed and killed in such a way every year. Spain puts the official number of bulls killed in official bullfights in permanent bullrings in 2006 at 11,458, but when you take into account the bullfights in mobile bullrings and the bulls killed during training and other bullfighting events, the figure is more likely to reach least 40,000 in Europe as a whole, and about 250,000 internationally.

Why do people defend it?

A continuation of the 'sport' has been justified on the grounds of national cultural heritage, some on ecological grounds, while others believe that it plays an important part in a country's economy. Such claims have been effectively refuted by animal welfare organisations, as well as by politicians and economists from across the political spectrum. Even Queen Sofia of Spain has expressed her dislike for the 'tradition'.

Some have defended bullfighting as a national tradition, seeking to preserve it as a piece of cultural heritage without which their country's identity would suffer. Nevertheless, many others have opposed it, recognising bullfighting for what is really is – a cruel blood sport causing unnecessary suffering to the animal.

Even if you believe that bullfighting is a tradition or culture, the fact that it dates back to prehistoric times and that artists have revered it can never really justify serious cruelty to animals. Cruelty is cruelty no matter where in the world it happens. Human societies and cultures have changed over many thousands of years, as has what traditions are deemed acceptable. Our understanding of animals has improved a great deal in recent times. There is no place in the 21st century for a 'sport' which relies on animal cruelty for 'entertainment'.

The ecological argument is also tenuous. The bullfighting industry points out that many fighting bulls are bred in semi-preserved areas of land called dehesas, home to several protected species and cared for as areas of outstanding natural beauty. The industry claims that these areas will disappear if bullfighting is abolished, because their business prevents the dehesas being developed for other purposes.

But the breeding of fighting bulls is not the sole purpose and function of this land, plus local authorities have never identified the bulls' removal as a threat to populations of protected species. The owners of the dehesas can choose to use their land in a variety of ways regardless of whether or not they keep bulls, and those that do keep bulls should be compensated for loss of activity. It is the job of local authorities to ensure that such land and wildlife is protected, and the necessary laws are already in place. Furthermore, the Foro Encinal, an alliance of twenty organisations whose role is to protect the dehesas, has never identified the breeding of fighting bulls as beneficial to the land's ecological balance.

Economic concerns focus on bullfighting as a vital part of the tourist industry in Spain; as a generator of money and as an employer of people. Yet, tourists will visit Spain regardless of whether or not bullfighting exists, and as people

become more ethically aware on their travels, tourist attendance at the shows looks set to fall even further. Indeed, a ComRes poll commissioned in April 2007 found that 89% of the British public would not visit a bullfight when on a holiday.

Like most industries, the profits from bullfighting end up in the hands of a very small number of people in a bullfighting elite. Even more importantly, the subsidies that prop up this declining industry take money away from serious social problems such as access to public health, education, infrastructures, the elderly, public safety, social housing and environmental policies.

An unpopular and unacceptable 'entertainment'

In Spain, the country perhaps most associated with the bullfighting tradition, a 2006 Gallup poll showed that 72.10 per cent of Spaniards were not interested at all in bullfighting and just 7.40 per cent were very interested; in Catalonia more than 80 per cent showed no interest at all.

Such statistics show clearly that the opposition to bullfighting is growing throughout Europe, and that it is no longer deemed acceptable for the

EU or for national governments to subsidise an activity which relies on animal abuse to make money. It seems undemocratic at best to use cash from the public coffers to prop up an unpopular blood sport, at the expense of crucial public services.

It is our responsibility to ensure that adequate protection is provided for animals in our care to prevent unnecessary suffering. I call on the European Parliament to reconsider the financial assistance given to the breeders of fighting bulls, so that the efforts to ban the 'sport' altogether can gather pace. The longer that bullfighting persists, the longer our standards of animal welfare will fall short of the mark.

For more information on anti-bullfighting campaigns, visit the website for the Spanish organisation Save Our Shame (SOS) or see the League Against Cruel Sports' 'Balls to Bullfighting' campaign to sign a world-wide pledge to boycott the 'sport'. *5 June 2008*

⇨ The above information is reprinted with kind permission from the *New Statesman*. Visit www.newstatesman.com for more information.

© *New Statesman*

Spain dies a death in the afternoon

By Vicki Woods

As a fellow-Lancastrian, I laughed out loud at the story of Frank Evans, the bullfighter from Salford, going back in the ring after a quadruple heart bypass and with a new titanium knee. 'I've tried retirement, and it didn't suit me,' he said.

Aye, well, happen. The leader-writer thought he was bonkers, but I think he has sniffed the wind. Bullfighting is on its way out in Spain, and he'll catch the last of it, if he lives.

There are so many polls charting the rising opposition to bullfighting in Spain that I don't have space to cite them. By age, the most opposed are the under-30s, by geography, the Catalans and by gender, nearly 80 per cent of women (including Queen Sofia).

Since women are now a majority in the cabinet, it's not surprising that the Spanish are going through their own anti-hunting/anti-blood sports struggles, as we did in 2002.

Which was when I saw my only bullfight, in August, on holiday in Andalucia.

By the time we came back in September, 'The Countryside' was marching for Liberty and Livelihood, my hunting friend was chaining herself to Parliament's railings and Tony Blair started wasting 700 hours of parliamentary time to ban hunting with dogs.

We met a history professor from Madrid, who had had a season ticket to the bullring for 30 years.

Juan-Luis, then 50, wondered if the proposed hunting ban would pass, and when I said yes, probably, he said that bullfighting in Spain would end in his lifetime, too. 'The King comes often to the bullfight in Madrid. One of the princesses comes a lot, too. Not the other one – she doesn't like it. Nor does the Crown Prince.' What about Queen Sofia? 'She never comes.'

He said, 'You must see the corrida before you leave Spain,' and when we saw a poster advertising a corrida at El Puerto de Santa Maria, he booked tickets.

It was so dramatic that I'll never need to see another. The first matador out was Ortega Canu, old, fat and nervous. The crowd yelled 'Maricon!' which translates (politely) as 'big girl's blouse'.

But Ponce danced with his first bull like an Argentinian tango champion. As he stepped and turned and brushed its body with his, the crowd began making a curious grunting noise – and that's when I got hooked.

I always thought *Ole!* was a wild Latin shriek, like those yip-yip-ai-ai-ai catcalls in the Gypsy Kings' songs. It's not. The crowd's *oles* were low, slow, gutteral growls, rhyming with 'holy' rather than 'olay'.

Step … *Oooooole!* Turn … *Oooooole!* Sweep … *Oooooole!* The growling only stopped when the bull finally stood still and a thick, echoing silence descended.

Flanks heaving, the bull stared at Ponce, and he leant over its horns and drove the sword into its neck.

When it collapsed, the crowd leapt up, cheering and waving white hankies (Kleenex, actually). 'He has an ear,' said Juan-Luis.

Blow me if they didn't slice off the dead bull's ear and present it to him, dripping. Not only that, he walked around the ring looking for someone to throw the horrid thing at, while people threw things at him. Hats, fans, pashminas, handbags. One man threw his toddling baby.

Well, he didn't throw it, obviously; he just ducked forward to grab the tossed ear, and the baby (perched on his shoulders) shot heart-stoppingly forwards and downwards.

The guy caught the ear and his wife caught the baby, rather niftily. Laughing, she then waved its tiny hands at the disappearing Ponce (rather than kicking her husband, as I think I might have done).

By the time Ponce got his second ear, Juan-Luis was in heaven. 'This was one of the best bullfights I have seen in 30 years,' he said, lighting his third cigar and settling back for what was likely to be an anticlimax: the most junior matador, Caballero, and the last bull of the day.

It didn't want to tango. It didn't charge, it bounced on all four feet after Caballero, turned in the air and

bounced back again, until it hooked him on a horn, tossed him in the air and trod on him.

Bulls weigh two tons. I thought the matador was dead, and wished I wasn't there. Half a dozen men raced out into the ring – including Ponce – to lure away the bull with cape-flapping, while others surrounded Caballero and made a stretcher out of their arms.

His head fell back and his face was chalk-white. I looked round for ambulances, paramedics, men in white coats holding drips and oxygen bags. None came.

Then he stood up, swaying, pushed away the supporters and called for a sword and a cape. His shoes had flown off. His backside was covered in blood.

The crowd was completely silent. Barefoot, he moved towards the bull's horns, leant over the top of them and pushed in the sword. Pandemonium. Hankies, fans, scarves – they tossed everything at him except (this time) babies.

I know, I know – you're upset for the bulls. I thought I would be upset for the bulls, but I wasn't. It's hard to say why, when I'm upset for every fieldmouse my cat tortures.

Maybe the whisky went to my head. Or the mob's bloodlust. 'They have a wonderful life, as young bulls, until

they're five years old, and then they have the chance to die so bravely,' said Juan-Luis's wife.

To say a bull dies 'bravely' is anthropomorphic nonsense: bulls have no human imagination and cannot do 'brave'.

She's from Arkansas and definitely on the huntin', shootin' and bullfightin' side of the 21st-century divide. But she was using the same language as those on the opposite side:

'How would you like being chased to death and ripped apart by a pack of hounds, eh, eh? Neither does the poor fox!' Does it? Who knows?

But the divide is widening and blood-sporters are shrinking, even in Spain.

Tens of thousands of countryside folk marched through Madrid this spring against the Law of National Heritage and Biodiversity, which aims to ban the lead pellets used for partridge shooting.

King Juan Carlos got into hot water when it was revealed that he opposed the ban. He likes shooting as much as bullfighting.

But there we are. Kings, huntsmen, blood-sporters, 65-year-old Lancastrian bullfighters – they're all so very last-century.

12 October 2008

© Telegraph Group Limited, London 2008

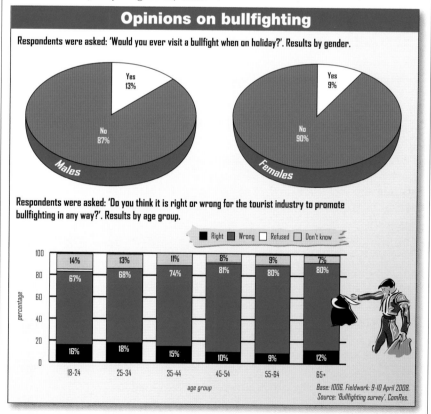

Opinions on bullfighting

Respondents were asked: 'Would you ever visit a bullfight when on holiday?'. Results by gender.

Males — Yes 13% / No 87%
Females — Yes 9% / No 90%

Respondents were asked: 'Do you think it is right or wrong for the tourist industry to promote bullfighting in any way?'. Results by age group.

Legend: ■ Right ■ Wrong □ Refused □ Don't know

age group	Right	Wrong	Don't know
18-24	16%	67%	14%
25-34	18%	68%	13%
35-44	15%	74%	11%
45-54	10%	81%	8%
55-64	9%	80%	9%
65+	12%	80%	7%

Base: 1006. Fieldwork: 9-10 April 2008.
Source: 'Bullfighting survey'. ComRes.

⇨ The DNA of gorillas and humans is 99.9% identical. (page 2)

⇨ Eight out of ten people believe that animal welfare is a key priority for a civilised society, according to new figures produced by the RSPCA – compared to just five out of ten who believed it two years ago. (page 4)

⇨ Worldwide, more than 40 million animals are killed for their fur – 85% are bred and killed on fur farms and the rest are trapped in the wild. (page 5)

⇨ Wild fur represents about 15% of the world's trade in fur. (page 6)

⇨ Today, around 400 designers use fur, compared with only 45 in 1985, and the fur industry is worth £500 million a year in Britain alone – and a staggering £7 billion worldwide. (page 7)

⇨ In the EU, fur farming is banned in the UK, Netherlands (foxes only), Austria and Lander in Germany. (page 8)

⇨ Animal circuses are much less common in Britain than in Europe. Although it is possible to watch acts including crocodiles, lions, snakes and even a kangaroo, a report estimates just 47 animals work regularly in circus rings in this country. (page 9)

⇨ An Ipsos MORI opinion poll in October 2005 for Animal Defenders International found that 80% of people agree that the use of wild animals in circuses should be banned – 65% thought that all performing animals should be banned. (page 10)

⇨ Intensive, indoor rearing of chickens provides 95 per cent of the birds we eat in this country. (page 11)

⇨ Around 70% of chickens raised for meat globally are raised in intensive industrial farming systems. This includes the majority of chickens in the UK, Europe and the US as well as rapidly increasing numbers in developing countries. (page 13)

⇨ The majority of animals used for medical research are rodents and all are bred especially for research. Of all the animals used, 84% (roughly eight out of ten) are mice or rats, 12% are fish, amphibians or birds, 2.1% are sheep, cows or pigs, 1.5% are rabbits or ferrets and 0.3% are dogs and cats. A very small fraction, less than a sixth of 1%, are monkey (primate) species. (page 14)

⇨ Globally an estimated 115 million animals are used in laboratories each year. (page 15)

⇨ There has been a significant reduction in the annual number of scientific procedures since 1976, this trend levelled out in the 1990s and in recent years there has been an increase in the number of procedures. Since 2000 the number of procedures has risen by 7%, with the rise in breeding procedures accounting for a significant part of this increase. (page 17)

⇨ Animal research has contributed to 70 per cent of Nobel prizes for physiology or medicine. (page 18)

⇨ An animal's body is actually very similar to a human's. Even mice share around 98% of their genes with humans, and most of their basic chemistry is the same. (page 19)

⇨ Most medical research – over 90% in cost terms – does not use live animals at all. (page 23)

⇨ Research using non-human primates is the most controversial area of animal research, but it accounts for a tiny minority of experiments. No great apes (chimpanzees, orang-utans and gorillas) have been used in experiments in the UK since 1986 and it has been government policy not to use them since 1997. (page 25)

⇨ 82% of males surveyed agreed with the statement: 'Yes, testing new medical treatments on animals is acceptable', compared with only 59% of females. (page 26)

⇨ A survey of over 2,000 people carried out in 2008 on behalf of the International Fund for Animal Welfare, the RSPCA and the League Against Cruel Sports found that, when people were asked about their views on whether fox hunting should be made legal again, almost three-quarters, (73%) said it should remain illegal. (page 29)

⇨ The Hunting Act (which bans hunting with hounds) came into force on 18th February 2005 after an eight-year battle that absorbed over 700 hours of Parliamentary time. (page 30)

⇨ 55% of people surveyed by Ipsos MORI in February 2008 strongly disagreed that people should be allowed to break the law banning hunting with dogs. (page 32)

⇨ So far there have been only two successful convictions out of 30 prosecutions for breaches of the Hunting Act. (page 35)

⇨ 67% of people surveyed in the 18 to 24 age group felt that it was wrong for a tourist industry to promote bullfighting in any way. This compared with 68% aged 25 to 34, 74% aged 35 to 44, 81% aged 45 to 54, 80% aged 55 to 64 and 80% aged 65+. (page 39)

GLOSSARY

Animal experiments
The use of non-human animals in scientific experiments, usually for the purpose of medical research. Scientists use animals to gain a better understanding of diseases and to test new treatments to see if they are safe for humans. In 2007 just over 3.2 million scientific procedures were carried out on animals in Great Britain.

Animal rights
This term usually refers to the view that as sentient beings, the basic interests of animals should be treated in the same way as the equivalent interests of human beings. Animal rights proponents reject the treatment of animals as property and campaign for their recognition as legal beings.

Animal welfare
This term usually refers to the view that it is not morally wrong for humans to use animals for purposes including food and medical research, as long as any unnecessary suffering is avoided.

Animal Welfare Act
Act passed in April 2007 which made owners and keepers responsible for ensuring that the welfare needs of their animals are met. Anyone who is cruel to an animal, or does not provide for its welfare needs, may be banned from owning animals, fined up to £20,000 and/or given a prison sentence.

Animals (Scientific Procedures) Act (1986)
Regulates the breeding and supply of animals for use in scientific procedures in the UK. Licences to carry out animal tests are only granted when the research is essential, there is no validated alternative to animal tests and suffering will be kept to a minimum.

Anthropomorphism
The attribution of uniquely human attributes to non-human animals or objects.

Blood sport
A sport that involves violence against animals: for example, hunting, bullfighting and dog fighting. Most blood sports are illegal in the UK – hunting with dogs being the most recent sport of this type to be banned (in 2005). However, hunting with guns is still allowed.

Free-range
Meat, eggs and dairy products which have been produced on farms in which the animals are free to roam outdoors.

Hunting Act 2004
The Hunting Act came into force in February 2005, making it illegal to hunt with packs of dogs in England and Wales. Hunting with dogs was banned in Scotland in 2002. The bill is contentious as it was rejected by the House of Lords and is opposed by pro-hunt campaigners.

Intensive farming
Intensive (or battery) farming involves large numbers of animals reared in a small area, often with low welfare standards, in order to produce high volumes of food and reduce costs.

Sentient
Capable of feeling pain and suffering and aware of sensations and emotions.

The three Rs
The guiding principles underpinning the human use of sentient animals in scientific research by replacing the use of animals with alternative techniques wherever possible, reducing the number of animals used to a minimum and refining the way experiments are carried out to make sure animals suffer as little as possible.

Vivisection
The act of operating on living animals by cutting into or dissecting them, especially for scientific research.

INDEX

Additional Resources

Other Issues *titles*

If you are interested in researching further some of the issues raised in *The Animal Rights Debate*, you may like to read the following titles in the **Issues** series:

➪ Vol. 159 *An Ageing Population* (ISBN 978 1 86168 452 3)

➪ Vol. 146 *Sustainability and Environment* (ISBN 978 1 86168 419 6)

➪ Vol. 144 *The Cloning Debate* (ISBN 978 1 86168 410 3)

➪ Vol. 140 *Vegetarian and Vegan Diets* (ISBN 978 1 86168 406 6)

➪ Vol. 138 *A Genetically Modified Future?* (ISBN 978 1 86168 390 8)

➪ Vol. 135 *Coping with Disability* (ISBN 978 1 86168 387 8)

➪ Vol. 134 *Customers and Consumerism* (ISBN 978 1 86168 386 1)

➪ Vol. 78 *Threatened Species* (ISBN 978 1 86168 267 3)

For more information about these titles, visit our website at www.independence.co.uk/publicationslist

Useful organisations

You may find the websites of the following organisations useful for further research:

➪ **Animal Aid:** www.animalaid.org.uk

➪ **Association of Medical Research Charities:** www.amrc.org.uk

➪ **Association of the British Pharmaceutical Industry:** www.abpi.org.uk

➪ **Coalition for Medical Progress:** www.medicalprogress.org

➪ **Compassion in World Farming:** www.ciwf.org.uk

➪ **Countryside Alliance:** www.countryside-alliance.org.uk

➪ **DEFRA:** www.defra.gov.uk

➪ **Dr Hadwen Trust:** www.drhadwentrust.org.uk

➪ **Farm Animal Welfare Council:** www.fawc.org.uk

➪ **Home Office:** http://scienceandresearch.homeoffice.gov.uk

➪ **International Fund for Animal Welfare:** www.ifaw.org

➪ **International Fur Trade Federation:** www.iftf.com

➪ **Ipsos MORI:** www.ipsos-mori.com

➪ **New Statesman:** www.newstatesman.com

➪ **Politics.co.uk:** www.politics.co.uk

➪ **Research Defence Society:** www.rds-online.org.uk

➪ **RSPCA:** www.rspca.org.uk. The RSPCA also have an extensive section on their website about their education work with schools, plus a number of available resources, at www.rspca.org.uk/education

➪ **YouGov:** www.yougov.com

ACKNOWLEDGEMENTS

The publisher is grateful for permission to reproduce the following material.

While every care has been taken to trace and acknowledge copyright, the publisher tenders its apology for any accidental infringement or where copyright has proved untraceable. The publisher would be pleased to come to a suitable arrangement in any such case with the rightful owner.

Chapter One: Animal Welfare

A moral claim to feel pain, © New Statesman, Gana the gorilla: grieving mother?, © The Scotsman, Animal welfare in the UK, © RSPCA, Animal Welfare Act 2006, © Crown copyright is reproduced with the permission of Her Majesty's Stationery Office, The fur trade, © Animal Aid, Fur fast facts, © International Fur Trade Federation, Fur goodness sake: skinned alive for the catwalk, © Associated Newspapers Ltd, Know the facts about fur, © RSPCA, UK circus animals given sufficient care, says report, © Guardian Newspapers Ltd, The cost of cheap meat, © Compassion in World Farming, It may be cruel, but intensive farming saves lives, © Guardian Newspapers Ltd, The five freedoms, © Farm Animal Welfare Council, Welfare issues for meat chickens, © Compassion in World Farming.

Chapter Two: Animal Experiments

Animal experiments, © Association of Medical Research Charities, What's wrong with animal experiments?, © Dr Hadwen Trust, Animal experiments – statistics, © Crown copyright is reproduced with the permission of Her Majesty's Stationery Office, Should we experiment on animals?, © Telegraph Group Ltd, Relevance of animal research, © Association of Medical Research Charities, Research and testing using animals, © Crown copyright is reproduced with the permission of Her Majesty's Stationery Office, The three Rs, © Research Defence Society, Animal testing – myths and reality, © Association of the British Pharmaceutical Industry,

Alternatives to animal experimentation, © Coalition for Medical Progress, Caring or cruel? Inside the primate laboratory, © Guardian Newspapers Ltd.

Chapter Three: Blood Sports

Hunting with dogs (fox hunting), © Adfero, Hunting Act 2004: the case for repeal, © Countryside Alliance, Hunting, © Animal Aid, Hunting after the ban, © Telegraph Group Ltd, Is the ban working?, © International Fund for Animal Welfare, Public opinion on hunting with dogs, © Ipsos MORI, Cut the bullfighting, © New Statesman, Spain dies a death in the afternoon, © Telegraph Group Ltd.

Photographs

Flickr: pages 3 (Marieke IJsendoorn-Kuijpers); 36 (Andrew Magill); 37 (J>Ro).
International Fur Trade Federation: page 6.
Stock Xchng: page 10 (Michal Zacharzewski).
Wikimedia Commons: page 24 (Carmem A. Busko).

Illustrations

Pages 2, 14, 23, 30: Don Hatcher; pages 9, 20, 25, 34: Angelo Madrid; pages 11, 18: Bev Aisbett; pages 13, 22, 27, 31: Simon Kneebone.

Research and additional editorial by Claire Owen, on behalf of Independence Educational Publishers.

And with thanks to the team: Mary Chapman, Sandra Dennis, Claire Owen and Jan Sunderland.

Lisa Firth
Cambridge
January, 2009